GRANDAD'S WAR

GRANDAD'S WAR

A C REYNOLDS

Matador
9 Priory Business Park,
Wistow Road, Kibworth Beauchamp,
Leicestershire. LE8 0RX
Tel: 0116 279 2299
Email: books@troubador.co.uk
Web: www.troubador.co.uk/matador
Twitter: @matadorbooks

ISBN 978 1785890 086

British Library Cataloguing in Publication Data.
A catalogue record for this book is available from the British Library.

Printed and bound by CPI Group (UK) Ltd, Croydon, CR0 4YY
Typeset in 11pt Garamond by Troubador Publishing Ltd, Leicester, UK

Matador is an imprint of Troubador Publishing Ltd

FSC
www.fsc.org
MIX
Paper from responsible sources
FSC® C013604

Dedicated

to

The brightest star in the sky.

CONTENTS

INTRODUCTION

Grandad didn't believe in God because of what he said he saw what other human beings could do to each other, yet my Nana believed in God because she said God helped bring Grandad home safely.

However they both had good hearts and believed in doing the right thing, they have taught me much and have shown me anything worth real value will always be attained through struggle, doing the right thing can at times be the hardest thing.

My name is Amanda Reynolds I'm one of Stephen Simpsons eight grandchildren, he was on the front line, 5th Battalion Coldstream Guardsman 2664217 Sergeant Simpson, he was an inspiration to me before I even started this project because he was always so jolly and warm and full of happiness, I said to him,

'One day Grandad I'm gonna sit you down and make you tell me your tale from start to finish on one of those Dictaphones.' I recognised his stories were in the thick of the action and held a heavy weight of importance and truth without my understanding why much more, I'm no historian with no particular interest in the war years, or I wasn't.

In 2004 I sat him down in his back room, the one used for best and guests at the home he shared with his wife Beryl (Nana) in Leeds, Yorkshire. Nana, kept us in good supply of tea and biscuits whilst I pressed record on my Dictaphone. My understanding and profound respect for my Grandad, his friends and comrades and the Coldstream Guards grew with every biscuit I ate, every cuppa we shared and every tape

I turned over for more, he is the only man I have ever met who can talk about the war and make it funny, even warm and comfy yet truly horrific at the same time.

I went away and asked the question,

'Is he just a gifted story teller?' I can tell you no, I researched for many hours and crossed off every date, every place, every name and I was amazed at the accuracy of his story, I even returned and asked,

'Grandad how come you remember everything so accurately and the day and the date even what the weather was like?' he replied.

'What was the last traumatic thing that happened to you?' I knew immediately what, when, where and how it made me feel, I understood his answer straight away, then he just carried on drinking his cuppa and whistling another little ditty to his smiling self.

I don't have a degree in history, but I have an interest in my Grandad's story been told so that my children and future generations understand the importance and atrocity of what happened during WWII. My hope is it will bring the World War alive to another generation delivered by my generation and should our children walk passed a cenotaph, they know what it represents and what war means.

The story is not full of facts and figures but has been researched hard; I have made sure it is as factually and accurately historically correct in honour and respect of every last man who fought for our freedom, in particular my Grandad's friends who died fighting.

This is the reality of one soldiers journey told from a true Yorkshire man's point of view with warmth and humour, quite how my Grandad made WWII seem cosy and funny as well as horrendous is a mystery. War is not romantic and they must not be forgotten, it's too important, it's too life changing, it's bigger than all of us.

This is a photograph taken of just some of my Grandad's personal artefacts that tell the story of his journey.

You may notice his medals in the centre, his green beret with cap star, his Sergeant Stripes and Coldstream Guards Shoulder Titles, a Nazi Iron Cross, some Francs, a Trained Soldier Badge and Officers Insignia plus many more.

Everything he kept is featured throughout his book, telling the story through pictures.

The Coldstream Guards motto is "Nulli Secundus" Latin for "Second to None".

1

'IT'LL DO YOU THE WORLD OF GOOD!'

Grandad, Stephen Simpson was a warm friendly giant, a strapping 6ft 2" and well built, he stood proud and tall with straight back making him appear even taller, his personality was as large as his stature. I remember hearing him before I saw him as he was always whistling a happy little ditty, when he smiled his eyes twinkled with an impish cheeky glow, as if he had one of his many rude or silly jokes on the tip of his tongue. He had great humility and loved his family dearly, with a forgiving nature and lot's of patience for his 4 children, 8 grandchildren and at the time of his death, 8 great grandchildren, still counting.

In an old Lloyds Bank security deposit box he kept an amazing collection of artefacts that he had saved, telling the story of his journey during WWII on the frontline. Through hard battles he watched his young friends and comrades perish, they never saw the future which their courage and lives helped to build for us. Be it strong spirit, sheer luck or tough fighting he was one of the few who made it home and made an unpretentious life for his family.

He was a founder member of the Coldstream Guards Association, Leeds branch and worked tirelessly for them all his life. His gratitude for the simple things in life and passionate respect for the forces taught me much, his recounting of his own story is warm, humorous and humbling, much like the Grandad I knew, I genuinely hope you enjoy it and take away with you a part of this everyday hero, who was a real pleasure to know.

My Grandad grew up in Garforth, a small rural village in the heart of West Yorkshire, England. He had a sister called Kathleen a brother called Len and his Father James, he lost his Mother at 14. When he was just 17 he went to join the army and escaped a life down the local coal mine in Micklefield.

When I was in the army we use to go down the front and there was this guy called Jim. But I will tell you about Jim, Bull Dimment later on, we just have to stay on the right line in the beginning.

From being a schoolboy I always wanted to be a soldier, on leaving school at 14 in 1938 I started working in a coal mine in Micklefield Collier.

When I left school, me two brother in laws were soldiers I'd always wanted to be a soldier, it was my intention.

Then in 1939 the Second World War broke out and everything went sort of weird in the fact that all the lights went out in the street, houses were blacked out, everyone was issued with a gas mask in case the Germans might use gas on us, this was at the beginning of the war.

I was 16 and went down to Little Eden it was on Marsh Lane in an old tenement building there, there were 3 or 4 recruiting offices in Leeds at the time, I reported there, I nearly got signed up for the Sherwood Foresters, the Nottinghamshire Regiment. The recruiting officer is looking at me, the Sergeant said

'How old are you lad?' I said

'I'm 18'

'Yer not'

'I am'

'Yer not how old are you? I'm saying you're between 14 and 16' he said 'I tell yer what lad, I can see your keen so go home and eat your brother then come back and we might think about taking yer on'

Towards the back end of the year I was fed up of working in the pit and I was thinking well this is no bloody life and I'll say this we were poor, we were ranked arse poor, this is no exaggeration, we were ranked arse poor and there were just me Dad and me at home.

My sister was married and me brother was away in the air force, my mum had died when I were 14 y'see, that were three years before like.

My Dad would be on one shift and I'd be on another shift and you'd get home you'd start getting a meal ready you'd start getting the water boiled up ready because there were no pit end bath in them days, you'd come home in your muck like y'see. In 1940 there was an announcement over the radio about Dunkirk, anyway well I thought there's a better life than this I'm going to try and join up again and I asked my father;

'Can I join the army?'

'Well' he replied 'don't be such a fool there's a war on. Keep working the coalmine.' But I was determined I wanted to be a soldier and protested.

'Well I won't stand in your way' he said 'but if you make your bed you lie on it and don't come to me squealing if the life isn't what you expected.'

He were hard were my Dad, he were as hard as nails, he was only a small fella, a miner all his life, his father had been a miner before him y'know like so you're going back hundreds of years like, a family of miners. I had no concerns, I wasn't an aggressive fighter but I'd stand me corner if it comes to it like y'know. I were one, well they say make love not war, when I went out boozing all I wanted was a good sing song y'know, I'd no aggression in me.

I went to join the Kings Own Yorkshire Light Infantry y'see, my brother in law was in that, so it was the drums and bugles what used to get me y'know, well even now hair stands up when I hear drums and bugles.

Anyway just before Christmas 1940 I went to the Army Recruiting Office in Leeds on Templar Street.

I saw the Recruiting Sergeant and he looked me up and down and said

'Now then my boy what do you want?'

'I want to be a soldier' I replied 'and I want to join the Kings Own Yorkshire Light Infantry.'

He started filling the forms in and took my name and so forth.

'What's your occupation?' he asked, I said that I worked in the coal mine; I wasn't a miner I worked on the underground haulage.

'Well I'm sorry my lad, it's more than my jobs worth, that's a reserved occupation I daren't recruit you, you have to go home and carry on working.'

'But I'm volunteering! I want to be a soldier.'

'Well I'm very sorry…' then he must have seen the disappointment on my face because he followed that with looking through his papers and he said

'Just a moment, there is a regiment that are recruiting for regular soldiers.' I said,

'Well how do you work that out?' he said if you sign on to this regiment you sign on for so many years either 4 and 8 or 7 and 5 y'see.

'You'll do 4 years with your regiment and if the war carries on you'll soldier on and then you'd have so many years on the reserve and you could be called back.'

'And what regiment is that?' I asked.

'It's the Coldstream Guards.'

'Oh I don't know about that.'

I knew they were very disciplined and what not y'know so I were aware of that and I was aware that young fellows out of our village, well there were 1 or 2 had joined and I'd spoken to them like, this was pre war and they'd come home in their fancy uniforms y'know like and they'd said it were murderous how they were treated. The difference between the Infantry and the Guards was that the Guardsman was supposed to be the elite and had really hard and tough training whereas the Light Infantry Man was reputed to be more of an etiquette soldier.

'Young man' he replied 'it'll do you the world of good.'

And his forecast was true, it did do me the world of good.

'How old are you son?' The recruiting sergeant asked.

'I'm 18.'

'And *how* old are you?' he questioned further.

'Well I'm 19.'

'That'll do' Said he 'sign here.'

I was 17 years old at the time, I was underage, I'd to provide references so I'd got one from a fella that I'd worked with at Micklefield Colliery and my head master and I signed on then for 4 and 8. I had to report for a medical examination which went ok and in early January I received my papers calling me up.

Anyway 9th January 1941 there were six of us joined up together, from Leeds area y'know and we were all sworn in together and travelled down to Caterham together. There was one fella Winston Burton, he was from Pontefract he was a painter and decorator was Winston and he was the old man of us like, he was probably 30ish and of course he was in charge of us like y'see. Then there were Billy Trotter from Leeds, there was Bill Fish, he came from round Barnsley area somewhere and Bob Fowler he was from south side of the county Barnsley way.

As I can recall it, it was an adventure for me, because I'd never travelled further than the East Coast, the longest trip I'd been on before was an evening trip to Bridlington, I hadn't been any distance so it was an experience on its own like y'see and going through to London, I was pleased, y'know been a young lad, I was pleased I had the older lad with me to take me through, I suppose I was a dependent sort of a bloke at the time.

When we pulled into London I was absolutely amazed at the damage round Kings Cross y'know the bombing the blitzing that had gone on because in our area we'd had nothing. I think one bomb dropped near the Woodpecker in Leeds there y'know and that was the amount of bombing at that time like, but I gather afterwards that we had one or two raids on Leeds.

It was a cold, damp miserable day y'know and seeing all this damage I was thinking I hope I'm not going to experience this like, all in my short sweet life.

There was a Salvation Army I think, they had a canteen sort of thing in the area of Kings Cross and we went in there like and they served us, we said we were gonna be soldiers like and they said they wished us luck and hoped we'd be alright.

We went right up from Kings Cross to Waterloo and then down to Caterham, we'd to make our own way up to the barracks, we got out at the station there and there was a policeman so we said,

'Excuse me we want to get to Caterham Barracks.' so he said

'Oh! You poor souls.'

What I was stood up in was what I had, I had 2 bob in my pocket and that was it I had nothing else, we were, I suppose we were all the same really. I wasn't old enough to shave so I had no shaving tackle just a towel and a bit of soap and that were me. So we got the bus, it was a dank miserable evening and as I say I goggled eyed it, everything was strange to me y'know like, we got to the bus stop up at Caterham on the hill, oh we'd Norman Bryant, old Norman, he was a case was Norman, and we got off the bus and Norman put his case down. We saw these big walls all around thinking it's a prison is this y'know and Norman sat down on his case and he got fags out and is having a smoke, I says,

'Come on Norman let's get in.' He says

'You gee up messin, I'm taking me time I says, cos I don't know how long it'll be before they let me out of there.'

So we all sat down and had a cigarette, our last as free men, it made me laugh, we reported to the Guard eventually and we went in and there was a Chapel at one side and Guard room at the other. We go into the guardroom and stared at the Guard who was a big outstanding Grenadier Guard, he was a

Sergeant of the Guard, I was impressed with him in so much that he was a big, smart, strapping man y'know and he'd a voice to match, he said,

'Now then what are you fella's wanting?'

'Oh we're Coldstream recruits.' I replied well he gave such a scream,

'PICKET SENTRY!' and this here kids flies in a bobs up bloody rigid y'know,

'Take these boys down to reception.'

Well he set off there his arms were going like a windmill and we were running and trotting at the back of him with our little cases in our hands and he says,

'There's a loony bin next door, I don't know which I'm in really.'

We stayed the night in reception, the following morning we were given a physical examination and then we were given an army haircut, this meant that you were left with a little tuft at the front of your head like y'know. Bill Trotter who was with us, had what was called the Boston Cut, this was a very long hair style, so Bill got in the chair and said to the Irish Guardsman,

'I'd like a short back and sides please.' It made me chuckle, the barber said

'Alright son I'll make it nice and neat for you.'

There was bloody hair all over the place and Bill finished up like the rest of us with a little tuft at the front he looked in the mirror and I could see tears in his eyes, it was funny. Anyway from there we had to have the dental inspection, when all that was done we were inoculated. From there we went to the Quarter Masters and were given all our equipment y'know, uniform, webbing equipment, all your pouches and what not, blankets, Rifle and a Bayonet which was the old short nosed Lenfield Rifle.

I had been in the Home Guard prior to joining the army so I had fired a rifle, it wasn't a thing to be feared y'know. The first time that I held a gun, actually it was a ROSS 300 Rifle was when they formed the Home Guard in June 1940 and I volunteered for it. I think we'd about 3 or 4 rifles between the whole squad so we use to take it in turns on Guard that's when I first started hold of a rifle and when I first fired one.

As a recruit at the Guards Depot like I say you were issued with a rifle, a bayonet and that sort of thing it was part of your equipment and they said it was your best friend. Well in later years I'd a disagreed with them because my best friend became me shovel, dig a bloody hole and get down y'see, so like I say my best friend was me shovel. It was a smashing rifle like and familiarity grew with using it every day, you'd go on the ranges and you'd fire a round or two. You knew possibly one day you might have to go into action, but you never thought about it and at that age you thought it was an adventure. Y'know you thought 'Oh Gun Ho! Lets go sort 'em out', you never thought of the reality.

You got use to it, it was a part of you was your rifle and as I say they did say it was your best friend I suppose it was in a way, but I still declare my best friend was me shovel particularly when we were in action y'know, active service.

Anyway from then we were formed into what was called a squad in 13th Company at Caterham, our Sergeant was Boxer Brown, Bill Brown, he'd been quite a good boxer in his time and was also what they called a Trained Solider in charge of the Barrack Room y'see, he was the one that would show you how to get your equipment together an all the cleaning an so forth. So after about a fortnight when the whole squad was assembled about twenty five of us with Sergeant Brown started the drill, the Foot Drill and then we went onto Arms Drill and then periodically we had an inspection. A four week inspection and then an eight week and then it came into the sixteenth and it was your final Pass Out. At the end of the training no body back squadded, in fact we'd 1 or 2 come into our squad that had been back squadded. Boxer Brown, he used to scream and shout at us but that was it, there was no evilness in it if you get me drift.

My attitude was this, I'd kept me gob shut and me ears open like y'know and say I made a mistake, turn to the right and I'd probably turn left he'd come over,

'You're a dozy fucker Simpson! Tell the squadron what you are.'

'I'm a dozy fucker Sergeant.'

It was just words; it was all part and parcel of the game. During that period of time you learned musketry field crafts and ceremonial drill and all the regimental history and anything to do with the regiment which was drummed into you y'know and if you were asked a question, you had to be on your toes to answer it.

On a night time on your bed, ground sheet were down and you'd have all your equipment in front of yer and trained soldier would be going up and down and you'd learn all your regimental history, the battle honours, the VC's.

They taught us the history of the Coldstream Guards; it was formed in 1650 at Coldstream and that's how they got the name. They were part of Oliver Cromwell's new army who were the protectors for England at the time.

They were based at Coldstream on the Berwick on Tweed border, in 1660 the regiment marched from Coldstream down to London to a place called Tower Hill where they laid down their arms, by this time Oliver Cromwell had departed the scene and King Charles II had come onto the thrown.

On this particular time The Coldstreamer's laid down their arms from Oliver Cromwell and took them up in the name of the King. From thence they have always been The House Hold Regiment along with the Grenadiers, Scots Guards, Irish Guards and Welsh Guards you see. Knowing the history made us exceedingly proud particularly when you passed out of Caterham as a Guardsman. There were no other Regiment like it you were the top one y'know, although saying this, a chap in the Pioneer Core would have that same thought about his own regiment.

I thoroughly enjoyed my sixteen weeks at Caterham although your life was very regimented and everything was laid out in order of what you had to do.

We were particularly lucky that we had a smashing sergeant who taught us very well and was a good trained solider.

Some of the NCO's were less than desirable, as I say we were very fortunate in having our particular one.

From there we went to Pirbright which was called the Training Battalion. Here you were taught firing on the ranges, lots of drill, then room marching and preparing you for anything and everything, preparing you for war like y'see.

We were prepared physically and mentally, but at the end of the day it was down to you when you were on the front line.

Regards lads fighting amongst each other, the first incidence that that came up and we hadn't witnessed it, there was a lad called George Cobby, (I visit his grave when I go over, he got first to be killed like, there were three of them killed together) George, he was a young fella like myself y'know and this Bob Fowler he was a bit sneery like and anyway when we come back to the billet Fowlers here was holding his nose and his eye was bunged up, he must have been onto George Cobby and George had given him a duffing like, well there was no more trouble. And I never saw anything, in all my time I never saw any bulling or owt like that.

During that period at Pirbright you were allowed to take specialist courses, these were the Mortar Platoon, the Signal Platoon, the MT Platoon (transport) or the Carrier Platoon, even cookery too. Well I fancied myself been a Carrier Driver so I took a Carrier course and you were driver and maintainer of the vehicle, a small track armoured vehicle. From there, after the period of training, in the October of 1941 the 5th Battalion was formed, these were all the roughs and scruffs from all the other battalions, the bad lads which they were pleased to get rid of, finished up in the 5th Battalion. There were chaps that had done time for burglary, fighting, been drunk and disorderly anything you could think of and one of these fellas had done it like y'see. You can imagine we were all sorts of scruffs and we were put amongst this rabble, it turned out they were the finest fellas you could wish to meet.

'When my Grandad remembered these men, he started to get upset and his voice broke. These were young men thrown together and became friends for life. His love and respect for these so called scruffs and bad lads of society was visible and illustrated his good and forgiving nature of people.

'Let me just compose myself' he said, and took a long moment of reflection.'

During this period the black out was in progress and in certain areas where there were static water tanks or big things like that y'see, just in case fire bombs were dropped, you were trained how to deal with things like. From there they decided, we were going to be an independent brigade and they were going to send us to North Africa, but then they actually decided they would form a Guards Armoured Division, so our brigade went in as Infantry for the Tanks and we were trained together down in Salisbury. Then we trained in different parts of the country, y'know, as a division, the types of country they trained us in must have been thought about, there must have been some marvellous thinking because after that training whenever and wherever we went in Europe we found ourselves in similar types of country y'see, which we fought across. Eventually after years of training all over the place after different kinds of training, landing the ships and so forth, beach landings and so on, we finally finished up in Eastbourne. I felt I was fully trained, they couldn't have trained me anymore, I did three months up at the School of Infantry with the demonstration section and we used to get all young officers from all over the country aspiring platoon, Carrier Platoon Officers.

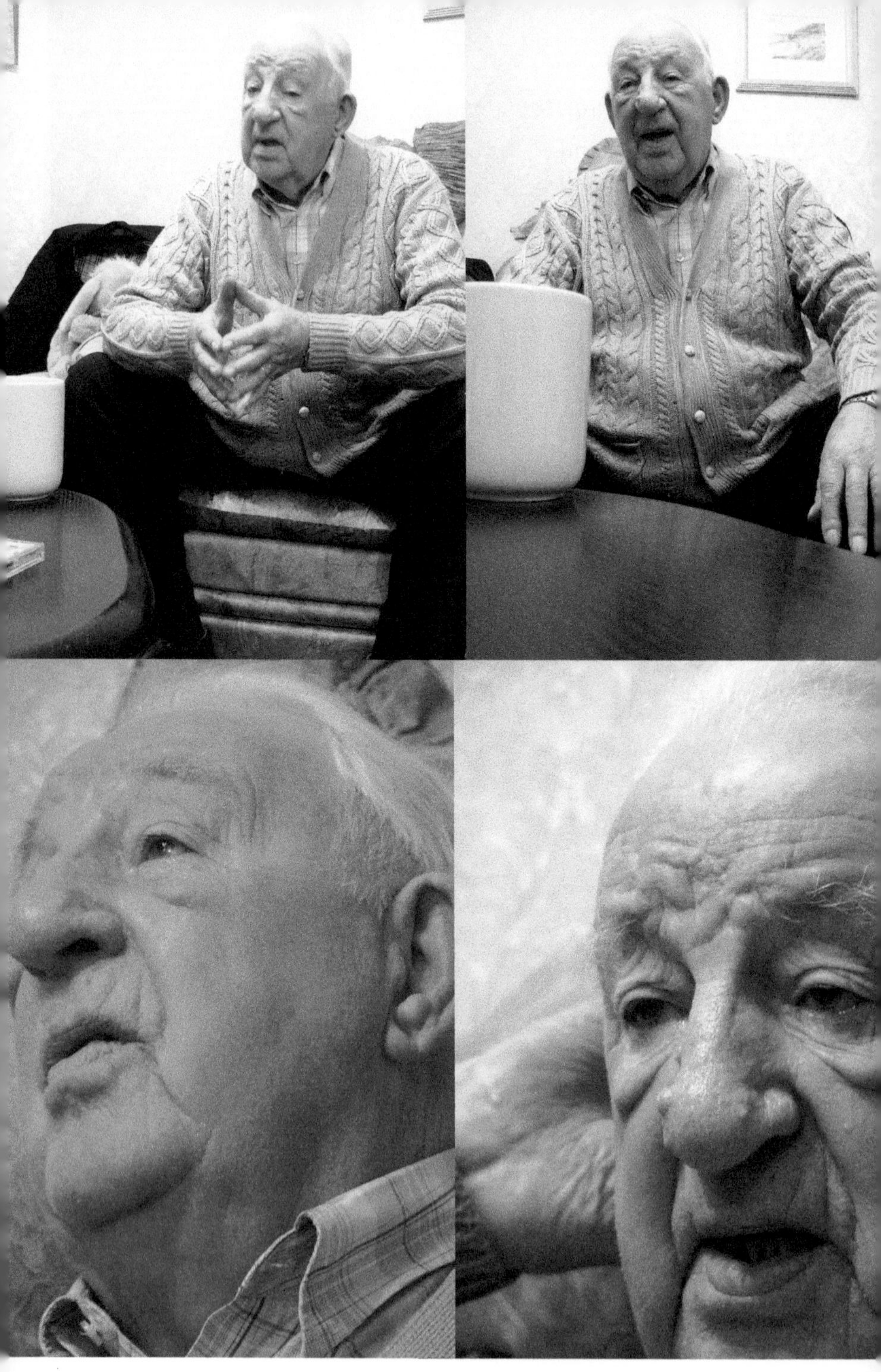

Steve during his interview

We'd start off first day and we'd get a crew, this is daily maintenance, and we'd go through the whole drill for the daily parade and maintenance eventually then we'd go out and we'd show them how we'd do a patrol and fire at movement and this sort of thing. And then they'd take the Carrier over, then one day one young lad would be driver and other Bren Gunner and they'd switch around then y'see and they'd go through all that we'd been showing them. It really was strenuous up there, hard and I hadn't worked as hard and been as fit in all my life I was really like a young bull then by the time I'd finished up there.

I did have the honour, once I'd stood out a little bit, I'm blowing my own trumpet now, I was told to report to the Officers Mess one day and I'd to pick two VIP's up to take out to the training area y'see, so I drove up with my carrier and who should come out but King Haakan of Norway and Lord Wavell and I took them out onto the training area and I'd to explain it to them, what was going off like y'see. So on my return King Haakan's body servant, man servant who was a Sergeant in the Danish Army and he saw me and he come out and he gave me half a crown and he said

'That's from the King, half a crown tip.'

'Grandad's voice is full of emotion and pride when he talks about this tip from the Norwegian King, it really was an unforgettable special moment for him.'

We got all the vehicles ready for landing and on the 6th of June we were ready to go and the invasion started.

It was absolutely amazing, that evening around a thousand bombers came over head to go over the channel and what a sight that was, it was a thrill to see them like, y'know.

So from there we moved up to a holding area in London at Wanstead Flats, it were a camp with a barbed wire fence around and once you were in there you weren't allowed out.

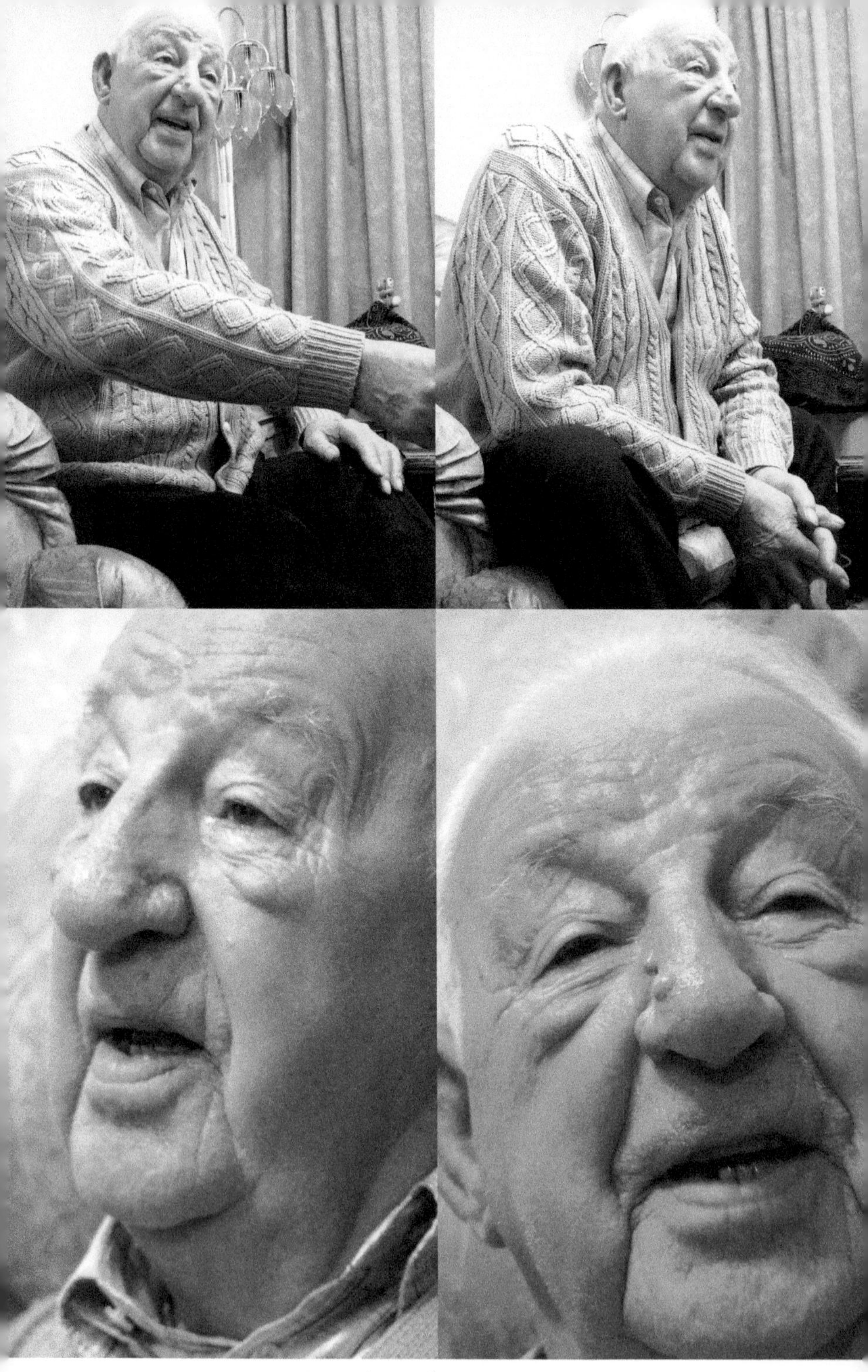

Steve during his interview

The instructions came through on what we intended to do and we moved from The Flats to The King George V docks in London.

'In 1942 whilst my Grandad was on leave he met my Nana, Beryl Clough, at Lillian and Johns wedding (friends of theirs. Throughout his time in the Army training and during his active service through Europe they wrote to each other.

Grandad posted gifts, post cards and greetings cards, she kept them and some poems and other items he had asked her to save, these were all kept safely together.'

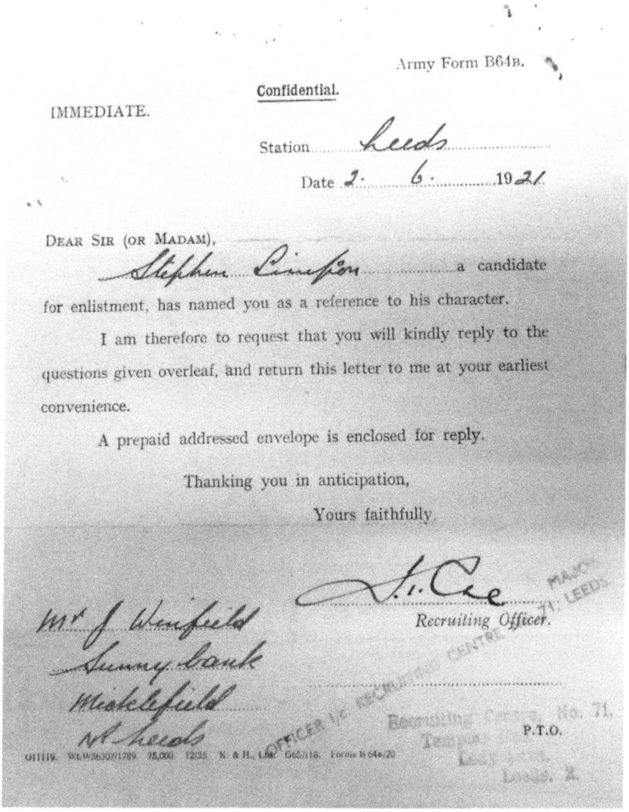

Army Form B64B.

Confidential.

IMMEDIATE.

Station Leeds

Date 2. 6. 1921

DEAR SIR (OR MADAM),

Stephen Simpson a candidate for enlistment, has named you as a reference to his character.

I am therefore to request that you will kindly reply to the questions given overleaf, and return this letter to me at your earliest convenience.

A prepaid addressed envelope is enclosed for reply.

Thanking you in anticipation,

Yours faithfully,

Recruiting Officer.

Mr J Winfield
Sunny Bank
Micklefield
Nr Leeds

P.T.O.

A Mr J Winfield, Colliery Management was asked for a character reference on Steve's application to join the Army.

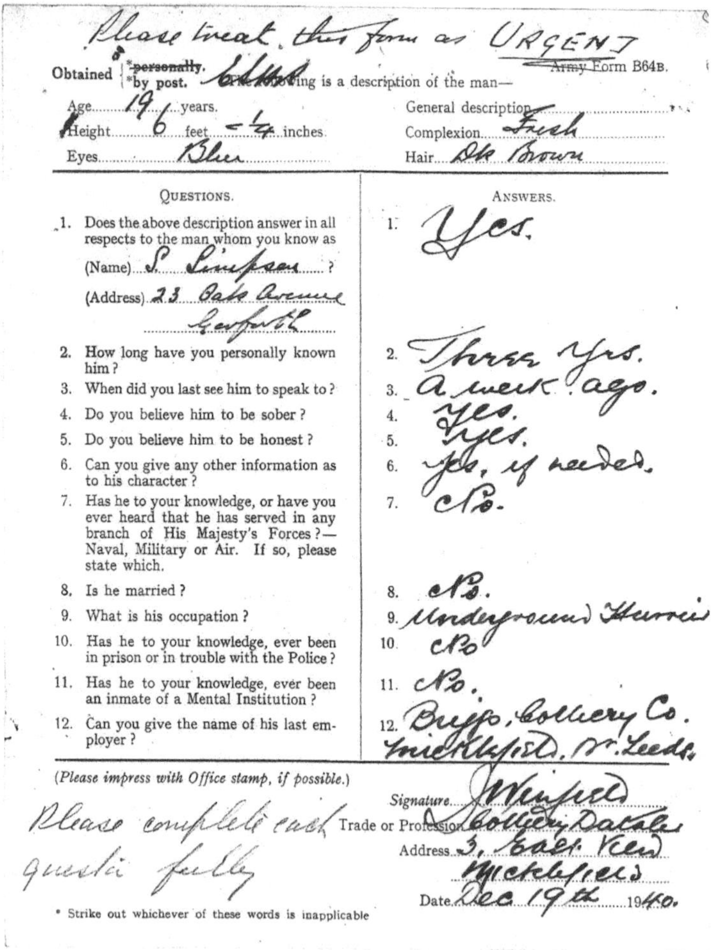

Please treat this form as URGENT

Army Form B64B.

Obtained *personally. *by post. The following is a description of the man—

Age 19 years.
Height 6 feet 1/4 inches.
Eyes Blue

General description
Complexion Fresh
Hair Dk Brown

QUESTIONS.	ANSWERS.
1. Does the above description answer in all respects to the man whom you know as (Name) S. Simpson ? (Address) 23 Oaks Avenue Garforth	1. Yes.
2. How long have you personally known him?	2. Three yrs.
3. When did you last see him to speak to?	3. A week ago.
4. Do you believe him to be sober?	4. Yes.
5. Do you believe him to be honest?	5. Yes.
6. Can you give any other information as to his character?	6. Yes, if needed.
7. Has he to your knowledge, or have you ever heard that he has served in any branch of His Majesty's Forces?—Naval, Military or Air. If so, please state which.	7. No.
8. Is he married?	8. No.
9. What is his occupation?	9. Underground Hurrier
10. Has he to your knowledge, ever been in prison or in trouble with the Police?	10. No
11. Has he to your knowledge, ever been an inmate of a Mental Institution?	11. No.
12. Can you give the name of his last employer?	12. Briggs, Colliery Co. Micklefield, Nr. Leeds.

(Please impress with Office stamp, if possible.)

Please complete each question fully

Signature J Winfield
Trade or Profession Colliery Detailer
Address 3, East View
Micklefield
Date Dec 19th 1940.

* Strike out whichever of these words is inapplicable

The reference given by the Colliery Detailer Mr J Winfield at Micklefield Colliery, Leeds, dated 19th December 1940. These are in his war record files at Regimental HQ, Wellington Barracks, London.

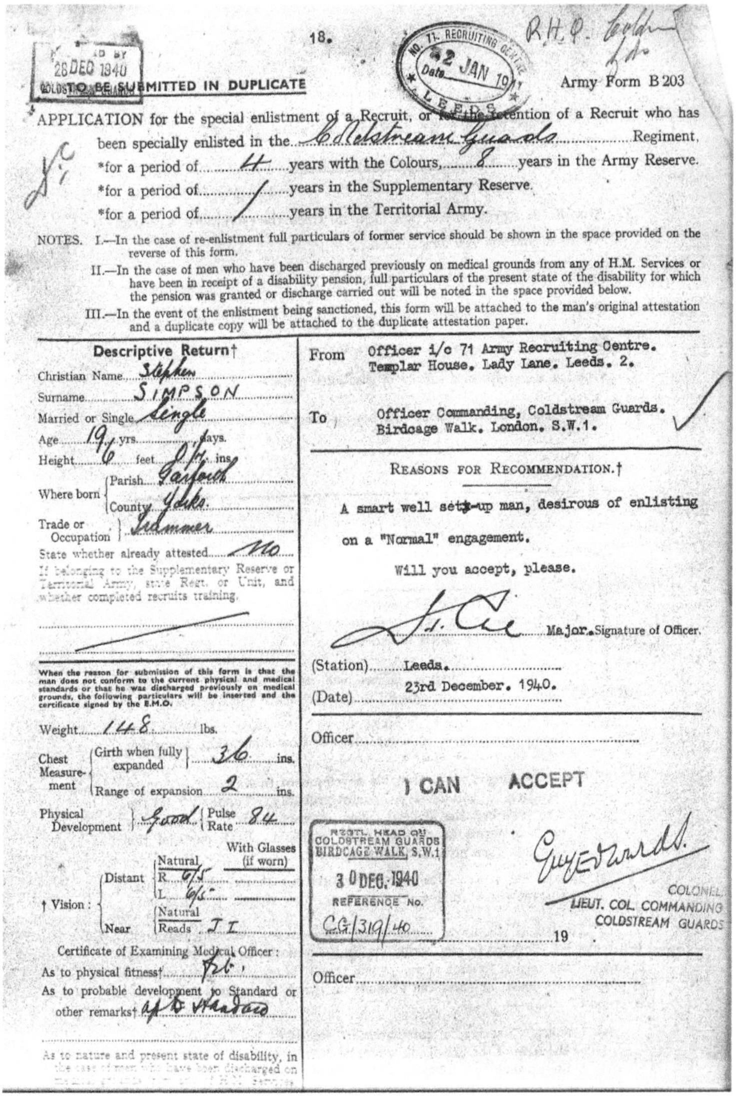

28 DEC 1940

18.

No. 71 RECRUITING CENTRE
Date 2 JAN 1941
LEEDS

R.H.Q. Coldm Gds

TO BE SUBMITTED IN DUPLICATE

Army Form B 203

APPLICATION for the special enlistment of a Recruit, or for the retention of a Recruit who has been specially enlisted in the Coldstream Guards Regiment,
*for a period of 4 years with the Colours, 8 years in the Army Reserve.
*for a period of / years in the Supplementary Reserve.
*for a period of / years in the Territorial Army.

NOTES. I.—In the case of re-enlistment full particulars of former service should be shown in the space provided on the reverse of this form.
II.—In the case of men who have been discharged previously on medical grounds from any of H.M. Services or have been in receipt of a disability pension, full particulars of the present state of the disability for which the pension was granted or discharge carried out will be noted in the space provided below.
III.—In the event of the enlistment being sanctioned, this form will be attached to the man's original attestation and a duplicate copy will be attached to the duplicate attestation paper.

Descriptive Return†

Christian Name Stephen
Surname SIMPSON
Married or Single Single
Age 19 yrs. 6 days.
Height 6 feet 0½ ins.
Where born: Parish Garforth; County Yorks.
Trade or Occupation Trimmer
State whether already attested no
If belonging to the Supplementary Reserve or Territorial Army, state Regt. or Unit, and whether completed recruits training.

When the reason for submission of this form is that the man does not conform to the current physical and medical standards or that he was discharged previously on medical grounds, the following particulars will be inserted and the certificate signed by the E.M.O.

Weight 148 lbs.
Chest Measurement: Girth when fully expanded 36 ins. Range of expansion 2 ins.
Physical Development Good. Pulse Rate 84
† Vision: Distant: Natural R. 6/5, L. 6/5; With Glasses (if worn). Near: Natural Reads J I
Certificate of Examining Medical Officer:
As to physical fitness† A.1.
As to probable development to Standard or other remarks† up to standard
As to nature and present state of disability, in the case of men who have been discharged on medical grounds from any of H.M. Services

From Officer i/c 71 Army Recruiting Centre. Templar House. Lady Lane. Leeds. 2.

To Officer Commanding, Coldstream Guards. Birdcage Walk. London. S.W.1.

REASONS FOR RECOMMENDATION.†

A smart well set-up man, desirous of enlisting on a "Normal" engagement.

Will you accept, please.

Major. Signature of Officer.

(Station) Leeds.
(Date) 23rd December. 1940.

Officer

I CAN ACCEPT

REGTL. HEAD QRS COLDSTREAM GUARDS BIRDCAGE WALK, S.W.1
30 DEC. 1940
REFERENCE No. CG/319/40

Guy Edwards
COLONEL
LIEUT. COL. COMMANDING
COLDSTREAM GUARDS

19

Officer

Steve's application form dated 28th December 1940.
It reads; Reasons for recommendation 'A smart well set-up man desirous of enlisting on a "Normal" engagement.
Will you accept please.'

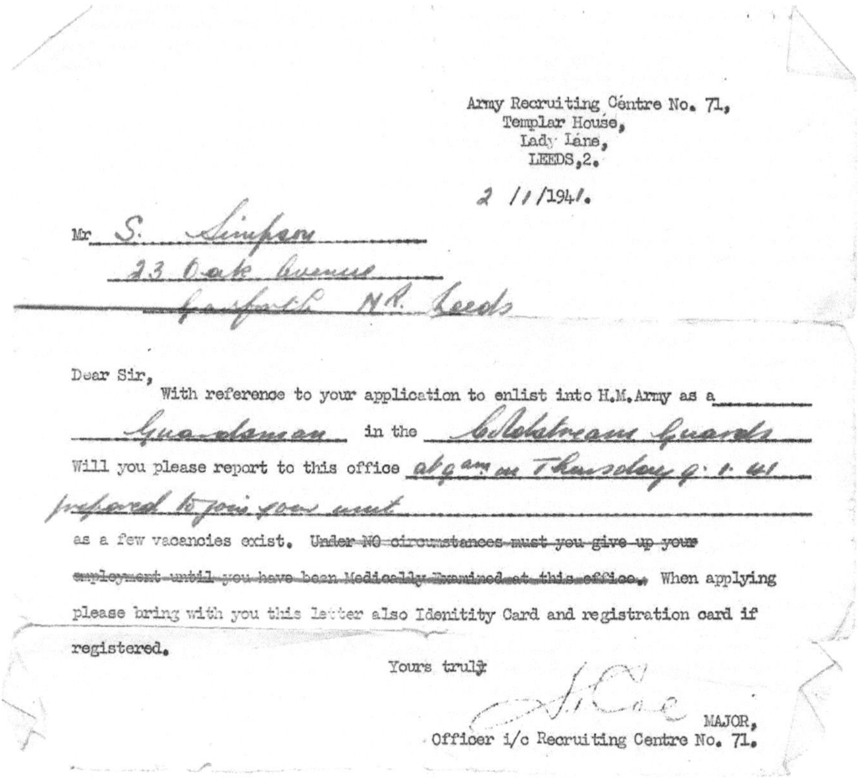

Army Recruiting Céntre No. 71,
Templar House,
Lady Lane,
LEEDS,2.

2 /1/1941.

Mr S. Simpson
23 Oak Avenue
Garforth NR. Leeds

Dear Sir,

With reference to your application to enlist into H.M.Army as a Guardsman in the Coldstream Guards

Will you please report to this office at 9 a.m. on Thursday 9.1.41 prepared to join your unit

as a few vacancies exist. ~~Under NO circumstances must you give up your employment until you have been Medically Examined at this office.~~ When applying please bring with you this letter also Idenitity Card and registration card if registered.

Yours truly

MAJOR,
Officer i/c Recruiting Centre No. 71.

Above: The Army Recruiting Office response dated 2nd January 1941 inviting Steve down to Templar Street, Leeds, to enlist for The Coldstream Guards.

Right: Steve's original Contract of Enlistment detailing terms and conditions for entering into contract with the Crown.

Army Form B 271A.

REGULAR ARMY. (All Arms.)

NOTICE to be given to a person at the time of his offering to join the Army.

Date -9 JAN 1941 19

You (name) Stephen Simpson

are required to attend *forthwith, or

at Recruiting Centre, No. 71, o'clock ....on the ....day of ....

at Templar Hse, Lady Lane, Leeds, 2. ....(here name some place)

for the purpose of appearing before a Magistrate or Attesting Officer to be attested for His Majesty's Army, in which you have expressed your willingness to serve.

The General Conditions of the Contract of Enlistment that you are about to enter into with the Crown are as follows:

1. You will engage to serve His Majesty as a Soldier in the Regular Forces for such term as is agreed on Attestation, provided His Majesty should so long require your services, with the additional liabilities specified in Question 17 or 18 on the reverse of this form.

You will be required to carry out the duties ordered by those in authority over you, and no claim can subsequently be entertained that you were enlisted for the performance of any special duties, or to be trained in any particular trade. The possibility of mustering a soldier into a trade depends on his passing the specified trade test, and the existence of a vacancy for a soldier of his trade.

2. Your term of Service will be reckoned thus:—

The service shall begin to reckon from the date of Attestation, or, in the case of boys, from the date of attaining the age of 18 years, but

If you are found guilty of either of the following offences:

(a) Desertion from His Majesty's Service, or

(b) Fraudulent enlistment;

the whole period of service prior to disposal of offence shall be forfeited.

3. You may be enlisted for service in a particular Corps or for General Service. In the latter case you will be appointed to a Corps as the competent Military Authority may think fit. Normally you will be enlisted into the Corps or Regiment of your choice.

4. If enlisted for General Service you will be liable, during the first three months of service, or at any time whilst a Proclamation ordering the Army Reserve to be called out on permanent service is in force, to be transferred to any Corps of the same arm or branch of the Service as that in which you are serving. In the case of boys, the three months period will reckon from the date of appointment to a Corps.

5. You may also be transferred to another Corps—

(a) with your consent:

(b) if you are invalided from Service out of the United Kingdom:

(c) if on the Corps to which you belong being ordered on Service out of the United Kingdom you are unfit for such Service by reason of your health, or are within 2 years of the expiring of your Service with the Colours:

(d) if the Corps to which you belong, while on Service out of the United Kingdom, be ordered to the United Kingdom or to another station and you have more than 2 years unexpired of your period of Service with the Colours:

(e) if you are guilty of desertion or fraudulent enlistment:

(f) if you are sentenced by a Court Martial to 3 months' detention:

(g) if while belonging to the Army Reserve you are called out on Permanent Service.

6. If you are now serving in the Supplementary Reserve or Territorial Army you will, on enlistment for the Regular Army, be deemed to be discharged from such Force. You will, nevertheless, be liable to deliver up in good order, fair wear and tear only excepted, at such time and place as may be ordered by the Commanding Officer, all arms, clothing, and appointments, being public property (including the property of the County Association) issued to you, and to pay all money due, or becoming due by you, or to be placed under stoppages until the value of such arms, [illegible] or appointments, not so delivered up, or such money is fully paid.

7. If serving out of the United Kingdom at the time you are entitled to be discharged, or transferred to the Reserve, you will be sent to the United Kingdom free of expense.

8. When attested by the Magistrate or Attesting Officer you will be liable to all the provisions of the Army Act for the time being in force.

9. If within 3 months of your attestation you pay for the use of His Majesty a sum of £20 you can be discharged, unless when you claim such discharge a proclamation is in force requiring the Army Reserve to enter upon Service with the Colours.

10. You will be required by the Magistrate or Attesting Officer to answer the questions printed on the back hereof, and you are warned that, if you make at the time of your attestation any false answer to him you will thereby render yourself liable to punishment.

Signature of the Non-Commissioned Officer serving the Notice } [signature]

* The Recruit is to have the option of being attested either forthwith, or at a future time. If he wishes to be attested forthwith, the words " or at ....o'clock on the..............day of......................" (in line 3) will be erased. If he does not wish to be attested forthwith, the hour (with the letters a.m. or p.m. as the case may be), the day, and the month will be inserted, and the words " forthwith or " (in line 2) will be erased.

TURN OVER.

CERTIFIED COPY OF ATTESTATION.

No.............. Name. Simpson Stephen .... Corps. The Coldstream Guards

§Regiment Selected.. §(To be entered in case of Household Cavalry only.)

Questions to be put to the Recruit before Enlistment.

1. What is your Full Name?.............................. { 1. Christian Name Stephen
   Surname Simpson

2. In or near what Parish or Town were you born?... { 2. In the Parish of [illegible] .... in or near the Town of Leeds
   in the County of Yorkshire

3. (a) Are you a British Subject?.............................. 3. (a)
   (b) Nationality of Parents at their birth?.............. (b) Father English Mother English

4. What is your Trade or Calling?.............................. 4. [illegible]

YOU ARE HEREBY WARNED THAT IF AFTER ENLISTMENT IT IS FOUND THAT YOU HAVE GIVEN A WILFULLY FALSE ANSWER TO ANY OF THE FOLLOWING EIGHT QUESTIONS, YOU WILL BE LIABLE TO A PUNISHMENT OF TWO YEARS' IMPRISONMENT WITH HARD LABOUR.

5. (a) What was your age (in years) last birthday?... 5. (a) 19 (years)
   (b) Day, month and year of birth?.............. (b) 2. 6. 1921

6. (a) Are you Married? (b) How many children are dependent upon you? } 6. (a) no (b) none

7. Do you now belong to the Royal Navy, the Army, the Royal Air Force, the Royal Marines, the Supplementary Reserve, the Territorial Army, the Army Reserve, the Air Force Reserve, the Auxiliary Air Force, any Naval Reserve Force, or to any Dominion or Colonial Force? If so, *state particulars of ALL engagements } 7. no

8. Have you ever served in the Royal Navy, the Army, the Royal Air Force, the Royal Marines, the Supplementary Reserve, the Territorial Force or Army, the Army Reserve, the Air Force Reserve, the Auxiliary Air Force, any Naval Reserve, or in any Dominion or Colonial Force? If so, *state particulars of ALL engagements } 8. no

9. Have you truly stated the whole, if any, of your previous service? 9. yes

10. Are you, or have you been, an Indentured Apprentice? If so, where? to whom? for what period? and, when did, or will, the period of your apprenticeship expire? } 10. no

11. Have you ever been convicted by the Civil Power? If so, give particulars } 11. no

12. Have you ever been rejected for enrolment or enlistment in the Naval, Military or Air Forces of the Crown? If so, on what grounds? } 12. no

13. Are you willing to be vaccinated or re-vaccinated? 13. yes

14. For what Corps are you willing to be enlisted, or are you willing to be enlisted for General Service? } 14. The Coldstream Guards

15. ~~If you are enlisting for service in the Cavalry of the Line, do you understand that you will be liable to serve with any Regiment of that Corps?~~ } 15. —

‡16. Do you understand that, notwithstanding you enlist for a dismounted Corps, you are liable to be trained and employed in such mounted duties as may be required? } 16. yes

17. Are you willing to serve upon the following conditions provided His Majesty should so long require your services?
   (a) For the term of twelve years for the first FOUR years with the Colours and for the remaining EIGHT years in the Army Reserve. If at the termination of such period of Service with the Colours, you are serving out of the United Kingdom, then for a further period of Service with the Colours of one year, or such lesser period as may be determined, after which you will be sent to the United Kingdom with all convenient speed to complete the remaining portion of such period of 12 years in the Army Reserve. (This sub-paragraph applies to men only.)
   ~~(b) Up to the age of 18 with the Colours and thereafter for the term of twelve years, for the first.............years with the Colours and for the remaining..............years in the Army Reserve, making a period of twelve years from the date on which you attained the age of 18 years. If at the termination of such period of service with the Colours, you are serving out of the United Kingdom, then for a further period of service with the Colours of one year, or such lesser period as may be determined, after which you will be sent to the United Kingdom with all convenient speed to complete the remaining portion of such period of 12 years in the Army Reserve. (This sub-paragraph applies to boys only.)~~
   (c) If, at the expiration of the above-mentioned term of Service with the Colours, a state of War exists, then, if so directed by the Competent Military Authority, to serve with the Colours for a further period not exceeding 12 months.
   (d) If, at the expiration of the above-mentioned term of Service with the Colours, you are so required by a Proclamation from His Majesty in case of imminent national danger or great emergency, then to serve with the Colours so as to complete your term of 12 years, and for a further period not exceeding 12 months.
   (e) If the above-mentioned term of 12 years expires while you are on service with the Regular Forces—(i.) out of the United Kingdom, or (ii.) while a state of war exists with a Foreign Power, or (iii.) while Soldiers in the Reserves are required by proclamation to continue in, or re-enter upon, Service with the Colours, and you, in accordance with such proclamation, have re-entered upon Service with the Colours, then to serve for a further period not exceeding 12 months.
   (f) If, after you have been transferred to the Army Reserve, you are called out on permanent service, then to be liable to be transferred to any corps requiring your services.

   17. yes

18. ~~Are you willing to serve upon the following conditions provided His Majesty should so long require your services?~~
   ~~(a) For a term of.....................years with the Colours? (This sub-paragraph applies to men only.)~~
   ~~(b) Up to the age of 18 years with the Colours and thereafter for a term of 12 years with the Colours. (This sub-paragraph applies to boys only.)~~
   ~~(c) If the above-mentioned term of..............................years expires while you are on service with the Regular Forces—(i.) out of the United Kingdom, or (ii.) while a state of war exists with a Foreign Power, or (iii.) while Soldiers in the Reserves are required by proclamation to continue in, or re-enter upon, Service with the Colours, then to serve for a further period not exceeding 12 months.~~

   18. —

19. Have you received a notice paper stating the liabilities you are incurring by enlisting, and do you understand and are you willing to accept them? and who gave it you? } 19 40 | Name Read | Corps [illegible]

I, Stephen Simpson ....do solemnly declare that the above answers made by me to the above questions are true, and that I am willing to fulfil the engagements made; also that I understand that, should my health fail or should I sustain an injury during service in the Army, I shall not be eligible for consideration for pension or gratuity on account of disability unless the disability is directly attributable to the conditions of Military Service.

Stephen Simpson .... SIGNATURE OF RECRUIT.

[illegible] .... *Signature of Witness.*

OATH TO BE TAKEN BY RECRUIT ON ATTESTATION.

I, Stephen Simpson ....swear by Almighty God, that I will be faithful and bear true Allegiance to His Majesty King George the Sixth, His Heirs, and Successors, and that I will, as in duty bound, honestly and faithfully defend His Majesty, His Heirs, and Successors, in Person, Crown, and Dignity against all enemies, and will observe and obey all orders of His Majesty, His Heirs, and Successors, and of the Generals and Officers set over me.

CERTIFICATE OF MAGISTRATE OR ATTESTING OFFICER.

The Recruit above-named was cautioned by me that if he made any false answer to any of the above questions he would be liable to be punished as provided in the Army Act.

The above questions were then read to the Recruit in my presence.

I have taken care that he understands each question, and that his answer to each question has been duly entered as replied to, and the said Recruit has made and signed the declaration and taken the oath before me at Leeds

on this 9th day of January 1941 ~~Signature of the Justice~~ [illegible] MAJOR, RECRUITING CENTRE, LEEDS.

If any alteration is required on this page of the Attestation, a Justice of the Peace should be requested to make it and initial the alteration under Section 80 (6), Army Act. The Recruit should receive a copy of his attestation on Army Form B 271A.

NOTE.—The Recruiter must erase Question 17 or 18 and complete the remaining Questions before handing the form to the Recruit.

* If so, the recruit is to be asked the particulars of his former service, and to produce, if possible, all certificates issued on Discharge, which should be returned to him conspicuously endorsed in red ink, as follows, viz.:—(Name)..............re-enlisted in the (Regiment)..............on the (Date)..............

NOTE.—Royal Naval, Marine or Air Force certificates are not to be endorsed.

‡ Applies to dismounted and partly dismounted Corps only.

P2917. Wt.W49241/2379. 75,000. 3/39. K. & H., Ltd. G657/51. Forms B 271A/17.

Left:
Taken at Caterham Barracks, young recruits Billy Wilkinson (left) and Steve (right).

Facing Page: Certificate of Attestation detailing all Steve's particulars including his false date of birth stating he is 19 years old when in actual fact he was just 17 years old.

Right: Stephen with his Sergeant stripes on his arm, a young NCO.

SGT. BROWN'S SQUAD 13th Coy. Coldstream Guards.

Mar. 1941.

Gdsm. A. Crane. S. Thomas. J. Morley. G. Douglas. L. Cope. P. Longmore. S. Simpson. W. Wigglesworth.

Gdsm. T. Hallas. W. Fish. R. Dobson. R. Fowler. J. Haigh. W. Trotter. J. Pepper. G. Cobby. W. Middleage. Lunt.

Gdsm. N. Bryant. W. Wilkinson. H. Burton. Sgt. W. BROWN. (Squad Instructor) T/s. G. Walker. Gdsn. W. Beechey. J. Shepherd. B. Wilson.

Above: Sergant Boxer Browns Squad. Taken March 1941 as the new recruits were just starting out in their army life. Gdsm A. Crane, S. Thomas J. Morley, G. Douglas, L. Cope, P. Longmore, S. Simpson, W. Wigglesworth, Gdsm T. Hallas, W. Fish, R. Dobson, R. Fowler, J. Haigh, W. Trotter, J. Pepper, G. Cobby, W. Middleage Lunt, Gdsm N. Bryant, W. Wilksinson, H. Burton, Sgt W. Brown, T/s G. Walker, Gdsn W. Beechey J. Shepard. (Squad Instructor)

Bottom Facing Page: Lillian and Johns wedding day, Leeds, Boxing Day 1942. A young Beryl is just visible 2nd from the left at the back, her face partly obscured by the tear. The back of the photograph reads 'Beryl, With love & Best wishes Lillian & John.' This is where Steve and Beryl May Clough met for the first time whilst he was on leave from training.

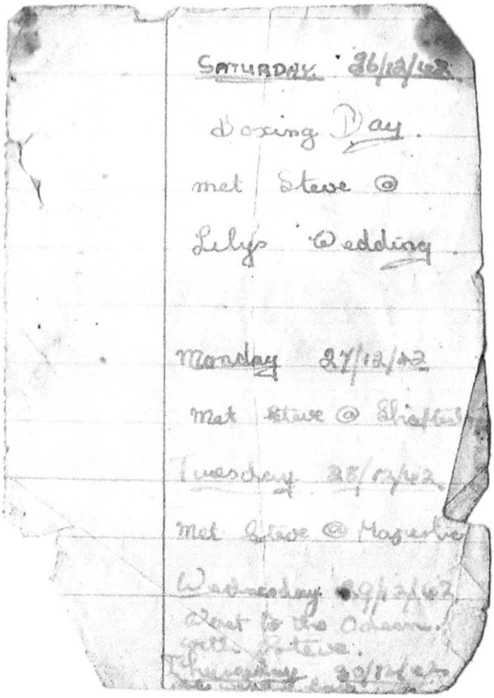

SATURDAY 26/12/42
Boxing Day.
met Steve @
Lily's Wedding.

Monday 27/12/42
Met Steve @ [illegible]
Tuesday 28/12/42
Met Steve @ [illegible]
Wednesday 29/12/42
Went to the Odeon.
with Steve.
Thursday 30/12/42
[illegible]

Above: Found amongst the collection was this small scrap of paper in Beryl's handwriting, it notes when they met and where they went for the following few dates thereafter before he returned to Caterham Barracks to continue his training.

PA

Army Form W.3017.

RECEIVED BY
23 JAN 1941
COLDSTREAM GUARDS

Report of Admission to, or Discharge or Transfer from, a Military Hospital.

Notification in respect of all Service patients will be sent as soon as possible in the case of:—

(i) Officers and Nurses (in triplicate)—Two copies to the War Office (Casualty Branch) and one copy to A.M.D.2.

(ii) Other Ranks (in duplicate)—One copy to Officer i/c Records concerned and one copy to A.M.D.2.

Officers i/c Records receiving intimation of the admission to a military hospital of Other Ranks from overseas whose documents are in their charge will immediately forward the Medical History Sheets to the hospital without waiting for an application from the O.C. Hospital.

Personal No. (Officers)
Service or Official No. (Other Ranks) 2664817 Rank Rct.

Unit or Corps Coldstream Guards.

Name (Surname): (In Block Capitals)	Christian Names:
SIMPSON.	STEPHEN.

Place, Unit or Hospital from which received, ~~or to which discharged~~:

Guards Depot, Caterham.

The full address (and code number) of the Hospital should be given.
It should be stated precisely whether this patient is admitted from (*a*) An Expeditionary Force; (*b*) A Station Abroad other than an Expeditionary Force; or (*c*) A Home Unit or another hospital at home. In the case of (*a*) the Expeditionary Force should be specified, and a clear indication should be given whether the patient is admitted direct from overseas, or from leave in the United Kingdom.

Date of Admission 19/1/41.

Discharge

Transfer from another hospital

Death

Diagnosis Influenza. Age 19.

Cause of Injury

Name and address of Hospital rendering report Military Hospital, Caterham, Surrey.

20/1/41.

Signature W.A. Blou[illegible] Capt. Date

(740) *M6701/367 350m(12) 10/40 JC&S 702

Below: Steve opted to join the Carriers division, here is a copy of his original licence to drive any vehicle whilst on Government duty. Given to him a few months into his training in the October of 1941.

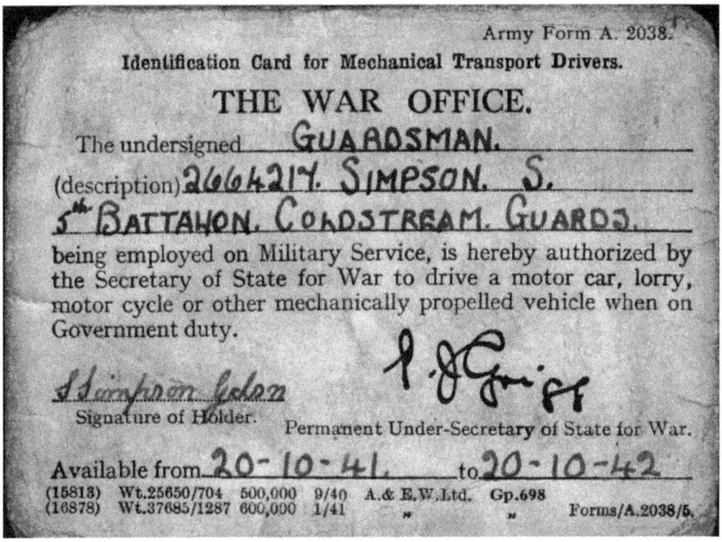

Army Form A. 2038.

Identification Card for Mechanical Transport Drivers.

THE WAR OFFICE.

The undersigned GUARDSMAN.

(description) 2664217. SIMPSON. S.

5th BATTALION. COLDSTREAM. GUARDS.

being employed on Military Service, is hereby authorized by the Secretary of State for War to drive a motor car, lorry, motor cycle or other mechanically propelled vehicle when on Government duty.

S. Simpson Gdsm
Signature of Holder.

Permanent Under-Secretary of State for War.

Available from 20-10-41. to 20-10-42

(15813) Wt.25650/704 500,000 9/40 A.& E.W.Ltd. Gp.698
(16878) Wt.37685/1287 600,000 1/41 " " Forms/A.2038/5.

Facing page: Found in his war records at Regimental HQ, Wellington. Hospital admission form for Flu whilst training at Caterham a few weeks after joining.

Above: This is Steve's original Soldiers Service and Pay Book, issued to him in his first year, it has recorded his details, vaccinations, employment roles, training courses and more within the Army.

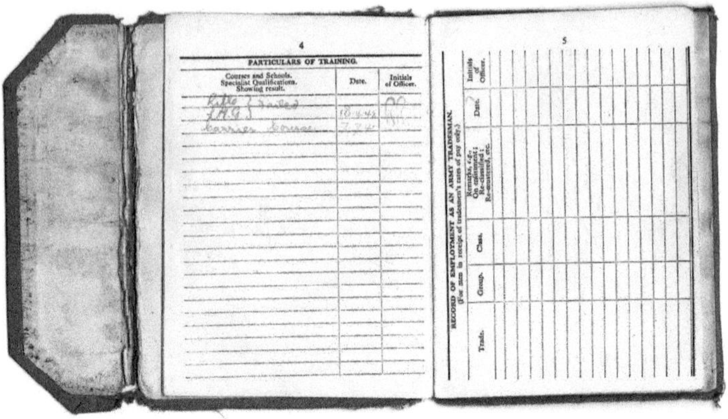

Above: This page tells us he passed his Carrier Course June 1941 but failed a Rifle course in April 1942.

Below: An original Permanent Pass, issued to Steve for after duties, he was permitted to proceed no further than London District and must be back at the barracks for no later than 23:59 hrs daily.

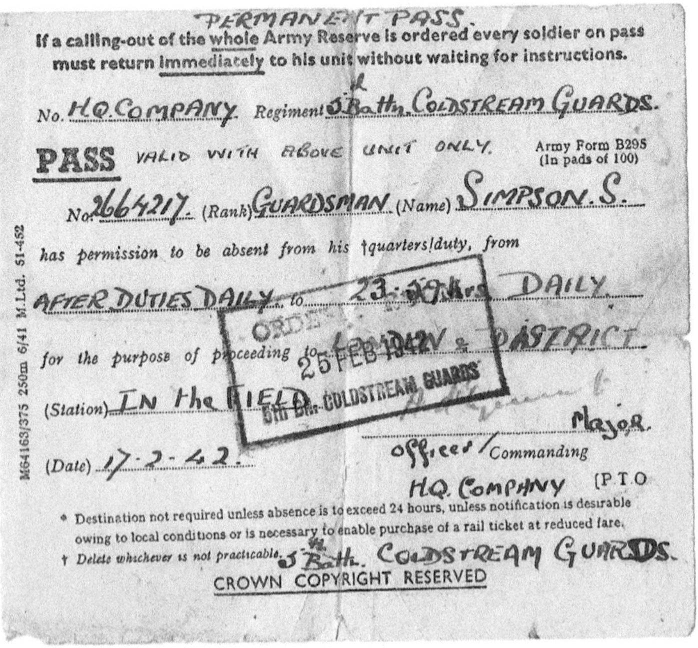

PERMANENT PASS.

If a calling-out of the whole Army Reserve is ordered every soldier on pass must return immediately to his unit without waiting for instructions.

No. H.Q. COMPANY. Regiment 5th Battn. COLDSTREAM GUARDS.

PASS VALID WITH ABOVE UNIT ONLY. Army Form B295 (In pads of 100)

No. 2664217. (Rank) GUARDSMAN (Name) SIMPSON. S.

has permission to be absent from his †quarters/duty, from

AFTER DUTIES DAILY *to* 23.59 hrs DAILY

for the purpose of proceeding to LONDON DISTRICT

(Station) IN the FIELD

ORDERLY ROOM 25 FEB 1942 5th Bn. COLDSTREAM GUARDS

Major.

(Date) 17-2-42. Officer Commanding

H.Q. COMPANY (P.T.O.

* Destination not required unless absence is to exceed 24 hours, unless notification is desirable owing to local conditions or is necessary to enable purchase of a rail ticket at reduced fare.

† *Delete whichever is not practicable.* 5th Battn. COLDSTREAM GUARDS.

CROWN COPYRIGHT RESERVED

M64163/375 250m 6/41 M.Ltd. 51-452

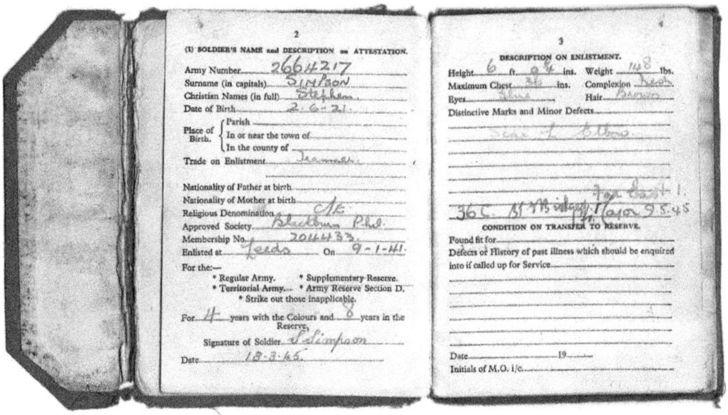

2

(1) SOLDIER'S NAME and DESCRIPTION on ATTESTATION.

Army Number 2664217
Surname (in capitals) SIMPSON
Christian Names (in full) Stephen.
Date of Birth 2-6-21.
Place of Birth. Parish
In or near the town of
In the county of
Trade on Enlistment [illegible]

Nationality of Father at birth
Nationality of Mother at birth
Religious Denomination C/E
Approved Society [illegible]
Membership No. 2014433.
Enlisted at Leeds On 9-1-41.
For the:—
* Regular Army. * Supplementary Reserve.
* Territorial Army. * Army Reserve Section D.
* Strike out those inapplicable.
For 4 years with the Colours and 8 years in the Reserve,
Signature of Soldier S. Simpson
Date 18-3-46.

3

DESCRIPTION ON ENLISTMENT.

Height 6 ft. [illegible] ins. Weight 148 lbs.
Maximum Chest 36 ins. Complexion [illegible]
Eyes [illegible] Hair Brown
Distinctive Marks and Minor Defects
[illegible]
[illegible] 9.5.45

CONDITION ON TRANSFER TO RESERVE.

Found fit for
Defects or History of past illness which should be enquired into if called up for Service

Date 19
Initials of M.O. i/c.

Above: Steve's Soldiers Service and Pay Book notes his birth date as 2nd June 1921 making him older than he actually was, his actual birth date was 2nd June 1923.

Left and Below: Steve's original Regiment Cloth Shoulder Title and Sergeant Stripes, he had kept both pairs.

Left: This is one of Steve's Cap Stars, worn on their uniform Caps, the middle section has been polished away and would have a cross on like his other Cap Star from his collection shown in

Below: Cap Star

Below: Trained Soldier Badge, issued on completion of his training

Below: Steve's old pin badge depicting the Guards Armoured All Seeing Eye Insignia.

Above:
All Seeing Eye, Shoulder insignia cloth badges representing The Guards Armoured Division. Steve was in the Coldstream Guards 5th Battalion, part of the Guards Armoured Division.

The two at the top are clean, a different material and appear unused. The bottom one is dirty, made from a felt material and appears to have been unpicked from his uniform, we believe this to be one of his original worn during service through the war.

This is the mailed fist of the 6th Armoured Division, this was worn in the UK where the division formed in 1940 and in North Africa, Italy and Austria where the division ended the war. We suspect Steve was given this back in England and then he was moved to a different company as they organised and changed the brigade from an Independent Brigade. He became part of the 5th Battalion which formed the infantry part of the Guards Armoured Division and 6th Guards Armoured Brigade who's insignia is the All Seeing Eye or Ever Open Eye, as Steve did not serve actively in the Mailed Fist 6th Armoured Division.

2

'YOU WERE NO LONGER A BOY.'

At King George V docks we boarded the ship and our transport and everything was put on, we sailed in the evening, we were ready to go, we were issued with 3 bags for vomit, a 24 hour ration pack, and an emergency supply of chocolate, it was in a tin and that only had to be used on the words of an Officer, you could never, y'know, you couldn't use that. So we sailed down the Thames and we anchored off South End for about 6 or 7 days, owing to the fact there were storms in the channels and such a glut of transport trying to get into Arromanches, eventually we sailed and landed in Arromanches. All of us were filled with trepidation at seeing all the damage on the coast and the signs along the coast road, Achtung! mines and so on. We harboured for the night near Bayeux, we slept in the fields and around the fields y'know.

'Amongst Grandad's collection of his wartime artefacts we found a copy of a document entitled 'The Brussels Sprout' Edition No.33. It is a war time newsletter dated 11th May 1945 and lists all the actions of the Battalion, in his own handwriting in the top left hand corner of the document is written 'Here's a diary of all our travels and actions.' *During research the document was confirmed to be a typed copy of the Battalions Official War Diary, the official war diary resides with the Coldstream Regimental HQ Archive. I refer to the document throughout the interview, a full version of the document can be found at the back of the book.'*

- The war time diary states it was the 23rd June when they arrived in Normandy to a concentration area south west of Bayeux.

  Brussels Sprout Diary

The following day instructions came through that we were going to relieve a regiment at a place called St Mauvieux in Normandy near the Carpiquet Aerodrome, we moved off in column, meanwhile the Tanks were still in England so we went in as independent Infantry. When the column were going in we left Bayeux and we were going over this rise and a short distance off I heard this 'ere squeal sort of noise, whistle and then there were an explosion and then another, I thought,

'Oh bloody hell they're firing at us! They must be able to see us.'

We took over from a Scottish Regiment who had had quite a pounding and had delivered the goods themselves like y'know. On our way in we were over a ridge when we were shelled, we started taking casualties as we were going in. It sounded like a thousand dogs howling in agony as they wound their thing up, all our hearts were pounding faster and faster, at those first moments you ever were under attack was when your boyhood left you, all your youth and silliness y'see it kinda went and you were no longer a boy. You can imagine been young fellas never been under fire before, huh, our skin was prickly and our hair was standing on end and we were breaking into a sweat not knowing what was going to happen to us. The CO's DR he were knocked over and we'd one or two casualties, anyway we got into St Mauvieux, this was all battered was the village y'know, they'd had the bloody flame throwers in and what have yer. It had been the Royal Scots Fusiliers that had actually taken this St Mauvieux village there was another little place, I can't remember the name and then there was the Carpiquet Aerodrome sort of thing over that side. We took over from these lads, we took the positions over and when I'd got me Bren Gun in, there were a lad that had been killed (obviously). He was laid on the side of the edge there and I thought well his rifle and bayonet were fixed, so bloody rifle I had you could have shot round corners y'know, it were a bloody awful rifle so I thought,

'Oh I'll swap it'

And I got his rifle and bayonet and there were one up spout like y'know, as I say there were one of the carriers, one of the bogey wheels, the rudder had come off the wheel, we'd got it stripped down, got it off and this was the same day and there were a bloody big attack coming in from, I think what they call the Vire area, it was further over, the bloody Tigers were on the job there, they were expected and we were going like bloody hell trying to get this 'ere carrier back together like y'know, with the prospect of Tiger Tanks coming, yer arse were going like that I tell you. Anyway fortunately for us the bombers went in and they really pasted 'em like, they knocked shit out of them like, they were hidden in the woods and what not, but we got through that. We relieved the regiment at St Mauvieux and we started having a scout around that evening, one of the lads said,

'Oh Simmy come and have a look here!'

And it was a house, it was blasted down into the basement and there were German bodies, the Wasp Flame Thrower which was mounted on a carrier had been in and torched the place like and there must have been half a dozen German bodies, SS they were down in this 'ere thing like, this was an SS infantry unit, these were the guys we were fighting in this area, they were evil bastards they were. The Northumberland Fusiliers were support troops, they had 4.42 mortars, the Wasp Flame Thrower and the Vickers machine guns, there were so many allotted to a unit, depending on what action they were going into like y'see. So as I say these lads had been in with flame throwers and had torched the place like and really that were the first time I had seen a German and fortunately the buggars were dead like y'know. What I knew about the SS before I came over was what I'd read in the papers, that they were a brain washed type of automaton like y'see. So as I say we'd taken over these positions like and we were told what was happening around us and me and another lad, I forget who it was, we were having a little reccy like sort of on us own and we heard this noise and it were like a thousand dogs in agony when they wind these things up like y'know, the moaning minis, the multi battle mortar y'know, you could hear the buggars zinging, like a zinging noise and after the first one or two occasions you knew exactly where the buggars were gonna drop, y'know, you'd a fair idea. Well this lot dropped probably 4 or 500 yards away did this here stick of bombs, of course my bloody heart were pounding, we didn't know what to think we'd never been told about owt like this, it were only through experience you got to know what the bloody things were like y'know, that was really the first time we'd come under fire. These moaning minis stood about 3 or 4 ft high and about 6 - 8 inches in diameter I think it was a 6 barrel thing they fired off and they'd drop in almost a straight line like y'know, so if you were lucky the buggars would drop away from you if you were in the shit the buggars would come to you like.

When the bombers came across, in your mind was the safety of the lads up there and what's happening to the poor buggars in the city itself like where they bombed, you were thinking of bairns, little children and women y'know, that were my thought anyway, but we were cheering,

'Go on. Get in there!' like as they came over but as I say you did feel for the civilian people.

Coming from a small mining community to seeing the bodies, flame throwers, war, it was a soul hitting thing to see, I mean it wasn't so much seeing the German soldiers, cos they were shit, but that were your attitude, it were when you saw your own lad, the feeling towards the Germans could vary depending on, because you were trained to get the person off, get the bayonet in, I suppose you got case hardened if you know what I mean, it were just another piece of meat you were going at but that didn't concern me, I was scared, I was bloody shit scared y'know, but by enlarge once you'd copped them, the ordinary soldier you'd kick their arse and say,

'It's over for you now, the war, lad.'

And we'd threaten to hand them over to the Russians and they'd shit themselves at that, but the first few lads you saw of your own, it got you, it unsettled you if you know what I mean.

· The 5th arrived with the Guards Armoured division on the 26th of June landing on Gold Beach. seeing its first engagement of the war against the Liebstandarte Adolf Hitler Division with heavy fighting at St Mauvieux.
History of the 5th Bn Coldstream Guards
www.5thbncoldstreamguards.com

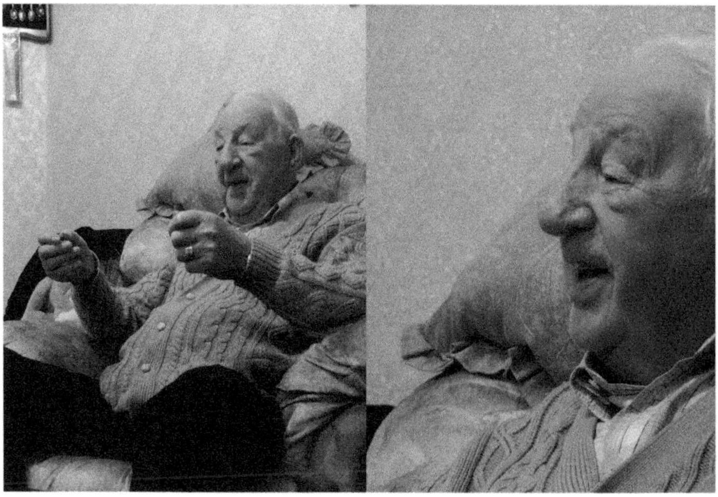

Steve during his interview

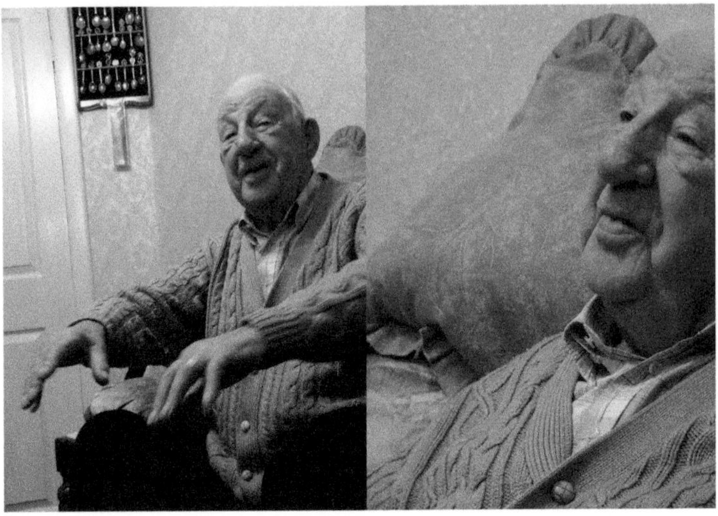

Now then it was a Line Regiment an Infantry Regiment we took over from, and of course of us been six footers or more, the trenches were very shallow, we had to start digging deeper so we could fit in, the thought still makes me laugh. I remember my first night in a trench, now you learn and I learnt very quick from the Germans, we'd gone into this position and we'd taken over as I say from the Royal Scot Fusiliers, now then over to the right there was a sort of rise and my mate said,

'Come 'ere Simmy have a look at this.'

And it was a trench facing the enemy, the German's one and it were facing the enemy so it were no good to us like but I learned a lot from seeing that, they'd dug their slits, they'd been in the houses and they'd got all the bed sheets outta the house and they'd put them all around the walls keeping it clean you see, all round the bloody walls they'd got a corrugated sheet in, a post in there and a post in there and they'd made a door, of course it was sheltered you see. It was no good to us though because our backs were to the enemy like but things like that you learnt from and figured out how to be comfortable. Well as I say the first night we were there, bloody legs intertwined and what not when it were our turn to go down and we just had blankets round us and I just thought,

'Well there's a better bloody system than this I'm sure.' So I said to Horace get your shovel and dig a bloody hole in't middle, he said,

'What for?'

'Let's put a bloody seat in…now sit down.'

'Oh aye it's alright is that' said he, so the first night in a slit trench Horace and I, (he was my Bren Gunner) we used to share a trench, we'd dig it in about probably 6 to 7ft, why we use to dig it so long was because you'd dig so far down so that you were breast high and then in the middle area you'd dig it out a bit further, probably another foot, so Horace would be sat at that side and I'd be sat here, so your feet used to go down in there y'see, so you could sit down.

While you were laid there, there were bugs and bloody all sorts of things dropping in the trench, little beetles and things, so next night I got my blanket I wrapped it round me and then the old gas cape, I pulled it up over the top of me like so I were in a sort of snuggy and put me tin hat on over the top, oh we were like little pigs in shit then like, it were lovely, you'd be sheltered from all the little insects and everything that were falling in, you could hear 'em pattering on you y'know and that's how you used to sleep when you'd chance to sleep, the blankets we were given were a coarse blanket and the buggars would stand up on their own after a while. Digging a trench was hard but I'd been used to hard work like y'know and it depended, in Normandy it were great for digging in because it was lush countryside you could really go to town with your shovel and as I say we learnt how to make ourselves comfortable so more often than not we were well away, when your exhausted you would just go out like y'know.

So here, well we were just holding the line in St Mauvieux and Carpiquet Aerodrome and the following morning we got instructions we'd to do patrol and I went on what they call Standing Patrol with my section of Carriers, we went onto the perimeter of the aerodrome we went through this little village it was absolutely obliterated and the riffle companies were all dug in all amongst the rubble like, Major Marco, I think he was No.3 Company, they were dug in, in this here area. When we did this standing patrol we use to have to go out at first light, just as daylight was breaking every morning and we use to go very quietly up this little track and get into position along the edge of the aerodrome, then at last light as it was getting dusk we used to pull back into the battalion area because we were forward of the battalion y'see. It was quite frightening at times because you were under observation all the time from the ridge on the far side of the aerodrome, they use to give us a battering with the Moaning Menace; it was a multiple mortar which fired bombs and you could hear them zinging, well after a while when you'd been peppered a time or two you had a fair idea where they were going to land y'see, they'd land and then there was an absolute tremendous blast from these things then they'd drop in a line.

We use to follow this track and we'd have a platoon from rifle company, we would be in extended order because the bloody snipers used to come in on a night so anything going up here we'd have a bloody peg at it y'see, so in extended order the drivers, as slowly as they could would drive us to the edge and then you'd to go round and to the track, it went right across the airfield up into the distance and round the perimeter and over there was a big chateau that the Germans had been using. Where we used to pull in, there were some bunkers built up and there were some bunkers at the back, the bloody Germans used to get into them at night, so it was a bloody arsehole twitching job was that. So you'd carry on round, infantry platoon would go back and you'd go and get the Bren's onto the 3 bunkers and it was handy because if there was any shit going down you could role down into the bunkers itself y'see, so me being Lance Corporal, young NCO I had to go into these bunkers just to make sure they were clear like, every morning, (I was made up in March 1944, before we left England I was at Scarborough when I marched in for my promotion) then we'd go in an extended line through all the woodland like and clear that too and make sure there were no snipers, all the woodland and trees were shattered everything you could see was, then we'd get into gun position and we'd be there observing all day long like.

We use to see the Typhoons had come in, they were the rocket firing planes and there'd probably be 3 at a flight of 'em, it was tremendous to see them coming in and they would dive right in and let their rockets away, we use to be cheering like mad y'know. There was one occasion where there was this water tower y'know with a bulbous thing, away out on the Aerodrome, we suspected that the Germans were using it as an observation post y'see, so one day the artillery opened up on it and with six shots they demolished this here thing, we thought it was marvellous shooting y'see so it were good.

- A month into its Normandy campaign the battalion had suffered 200 casualties, killed and wounded.
  History of the 5th Bn Coldstream Guards
  www.5thbncoldstreamguards.com

Your nerves were jangling all the time, you were wandering 'Am I gonna get through this' y'know like, some chaps did go, their nerves just went, there were quite a number, personally I was frightened, funnily enough I thought,

'Well I don't want to be, or to look a coward in front of me mates.'

'Grandad got upset at this point during the interview, his voice started to break at the memory of been so frightened yet trying to remain strong for himself and the others around him who looked up to him for support. After a long pause he continued.'

So I was an NCO then and it were up to me to show that we could do things, well I started up as a Lance Corporal the lowest, then I became a Lance Sergeant, not particularly through merit but because a lot of the people were getting knocked over and promotion came very fast, then I finished up as a full Sergeant which meant I had more responsibility for other people than I had for myself like y'see. I was proud to be a Sergeant and I had respect from below me and above, so it was a great rank to have I thought, at times depending who it was I'd have to give 'em a right good bollocking, or if I knew they were a sensitive lad I'd say,

'Come 'ere old mate have a fag let's talk about it.'

When there was a threat to life I got lads to do things they had to do, I suppose I was a silly buggar, if I were told to do something, irrespective I'd make an attempt to do it and the lads that were with me, they knew my nature and I use to say to them,

'Look I don't want to be the one that's Yella round here, are you going to join me?' y'know if it was shitty job to do I'd lead by example. Well as I say I was the boss man I had to show them that we had to do it, or we could do it like y'know, on my crew they were buggars, they were 3 smashers y'know, there was Horace, Horace Camm was me Bren Gunner he was a boy, a Doncaster lad, nowadays they'd say he was thick, he had no nerves at all that fella, looking back all I can think is he must have been a bit thick as well, he was a smashing lad, he was a right good looter he had a nose for anything to be scrounged, if it were to be had Horace would scrounge it like y'know. I think I were a good NCO, I had a driver called Peacock he was a baby faced little lad from Brighton, little Peacock, I never knew his first name but he was a lad, Charlie Coverdale from Harrogate he was my observer and mortar man and they were alright, they'd do anything I'd ask them to do, they'd go anywhere where I went like y'know and young Peacock, he was a little hero, I used to curse him and kick his arse on y'know and he was there with me, if a shell was ages away he'd start, y'know getting nervous and I used to say,

'Get your bloody cigs going, get in that trench outta road like' y'know.

'Grandad's voice filled up with emotion as he spoke about his role as NCO when he talked about his crew he welled up remembering his comrades so fondly, at the mention of Horace's name Grandad got really upset, but he carried on and a fond smile and a chuckle omitted from Grandad and he laughed warmly at Horace. When he talked about young Peacock he just broke down and started to cry.'

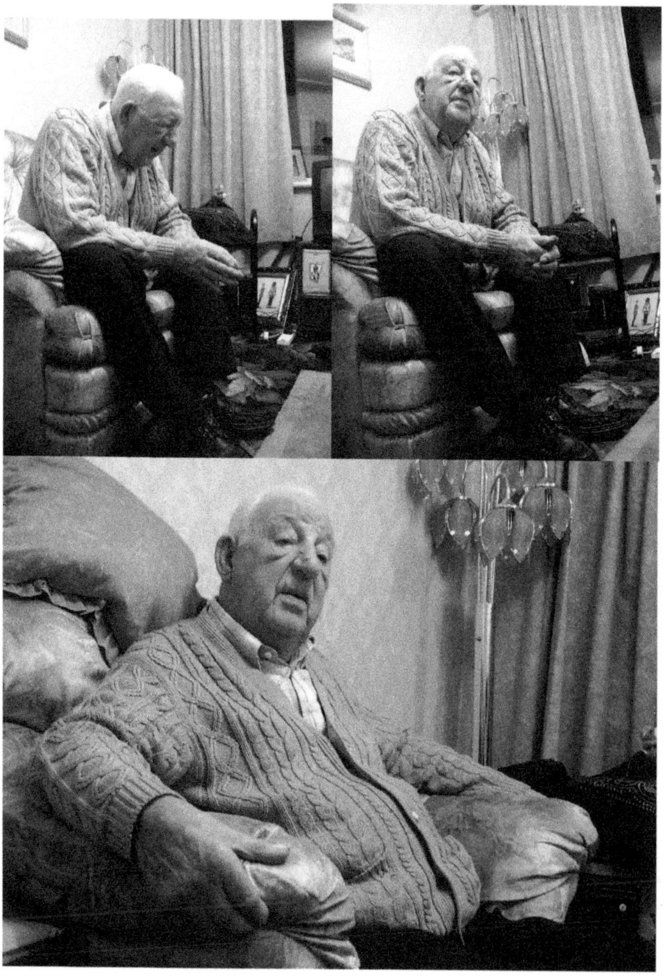

Steve during his interview

A sniper can pick a man off at 1000m, the only experience I had with a sniper, I'm jumping ahead of us like but when we'd done the 3 Armoured Division, the Tanks, we got down to Cagney and we dug in and took over some of the German positions for the night, then the following day there was a bloody 88 firing across the front and there were tanks going up left right and centre. There was a platoon dug in over there and Captain Fanning was down at the side of this here wall with the carrier and wireless like, he said,

'Officer Simpson I want you to go over to that platoon and see if they can spot this gun and where its firing from.'

So I'm going up this edge side and there were some premonition 'Hit the deck Simmy' and as I hit the deck, he must have spotted me this fucking sniper like, I hit the deck and I heard the crack boom y'know and I set off crawling, it was a bloody potato field and I crawled up like and I got in touch with the platoon and I heard Captain Fanning,

'Are you alright, are you alright Simpson?' and I said

'Yeah I'm ok Sir.'

But coming back I didn't expose myself, I were down in't bloody tateys, like I say that was the only time I was fired at by a sniper.

More often than not things turned out ok, sometimes you did have to say to your Officers,

'I'm afraid this lad won't make it I'd be better off with out him.'

And they'd move him out like, it was very, very rarely it happened, there was one incident when it did happen, he was an airport man he was a Sergeant fella.

'Grandad asked that I remove the name of the Sergeant he talks about next as he did not want to offend or disrespect the man's family.'

It was after the 3 Armoured Divisions had put down their

advance we got as far down as a place called Cagney, there was this ridge and it was lined with 88's and there were no way that our tanks were going to get through there, no way. There were 400 tanks knocked out in that 2 day action, you can imagine what was going off and this particular morning there were 2 sections of us and this is where that Sergeant A, he was yellow was this man. Anyway this was the first time I'd come under personal fire like and Captain Fanning had ordered 2 sections of us, that was 8 of us, to this strip of orchard that had been badly shelled, well all the area had been bombed and almost obliterated y'know, it was like one of the first world war scenes, so they suspected this gun was up in this wood here somewhere, so we were in extended order. I was over one side with my lads and Sergeant A was over at the other side, well he should have been, we got so far in and he's was almost literally hanging onto me,

'I can't stand this Simmy, I can't stand this Simmy.'

He's saying and I played blind and I told him to F' Off like and get with his lads. He was a type of fella who was a bully when we were serving in England y'know, there were no give or take with him and he were yellow, he use to give us a dog's life when we were in England training, a nasty person he was nobody had any respect for him, anyway I saw the Officer after and said,

'Get him out, he's shit is this man.'

And he did, kicked him out straight away, as I say though you'd get other fellas and they tried to keep going, but their nerves would go and they were genuine, where as this fella, he was yella, gutless and a bully. Anyway we were going up this orchard and a burst of fire came over the top of us like y'know and we all hit the deck and as we were going on through, there was a dug out and I think it must have been a command post for their artillery because there were all sorts of gear in it. We went in and I regret to this day, I knew I should of brought it, there was their maps of the area and on the reverse it said Sea

Lion it were part of the British course for when the Germans were gonna do their invasion and they'd reversed the sign and put Normandy on and I bitterly regret I never brought any for a souvenir like. Anyway we got this buggar, there were 3 of them we sorted them out we slung a bloody grenade over and we got 1 of them and then I think one of the lads shot 1 of them and t'other buggar gave himself up like y'see. So we'd stopped the bloody sniper, I don't know what happened about the 88, that kept on firing.

I'd been on't go in all the actions from us landing like, I'd taken part in them so old Captain Fanning, he must have taken a shine to me I got on bloody well with him, I'll tell you a little incident, I volunteered for commandos December of 1943 back in England, there were about 20 of us from our battalions, 2 or 3 of us from our company and we went through to Scarborough and saw the Commando Officer, he interviewed us and we had a medical and he looked at us and said,

'Now then if you're due for leave you've to tell your unit you've to be back at Acknar Carry on 7th January.'

So I went home, I had Christmas at home like and it brought us up to New Years Eve and I were due to go back and a mate of mine he was on draft leave and he were due to go to Burma, I met him so we went on't pop like and had another day at home, anyway of course we were arrested and marched under Company Orders, we were out at Drighlington, and marched in and the Officer says,

'Right extra service, been absent from duty, what do you have to say Sir?'

'Nothing Sir.' I said, he said

'Well I've got something to say. I thought you were going to the commandos aren't you?'

'I am Sir.'

'Well I've got news for you; Captain Fanning has had your transfer stopped.'

He'd been away when I'd applied for the commandos had Cpt. Fanning and soon as he'd come back and found out I was joining the commandos he'd got my transfer stopped. He, Captain Fanning had a little Billet a little hut nearby so as I come out he's happened to be just coming down the lane he says,

'Go away, go away, you'll thank me one day Simpson now go away.'

That were Percy fanning, I think he didn't want to lose one of his best soldier's maybe.

There were some characters, Norman Bryant he was another one, he was a Castleford Collier lad, hard as nails, he'd been a Yorkshire Boy champion boxer and you could tell it, he played rugby and boxing, he'd 2 or 3 teeth at the front y'know.

'Grandad chuckled fondly at the memory of Norman Bryant.'

He was a character was Norman and one night, young recruits y'know what you're like, you were hungry, you'd had your tea it got to about 8oclock and you were all starving so were all there moaning and old Norman, said,

'What on earths wrong with yer old long legs?'

'Were all starving' I replied, he says

'Get that stove going get it red hot' and off he goes like, and he comes back about half an hour later and his blouse were bulging, he'd bloody sausage bacon, bread, margarine, he'd the lot in there, he said,

'Get your messing out.' We'd a big fry up, we says,

'Where'd you get that from?'

'Never mind where I got that from' he says 'Manna from heaven.'

Anyway next morning there were hell on in 13th Company lines, bloody sergeants mess had been broken into, cook house, an all the bloody breakfast had been nicked and we'd bloody scoffed it and it was Norman, he were that type of fella y'know.

One St Georges Day and the Sergeants had been off to a dance in the afternoon, what with bombing raids on a night like y'know and they had their dance in the gym like up at the depot. So our squad were detailed off afterward to go and scrub the bloody floor so it was all ready again, it was about 7oclock in the evening we were up there, I was with my old bucket and Mick says,

'Work your way up into that corner.'

There were a bloody table with all the bloody bottles of hooch and what not, so I put a bottle of whiskey in my bucket and scrubbed me way out t'door.

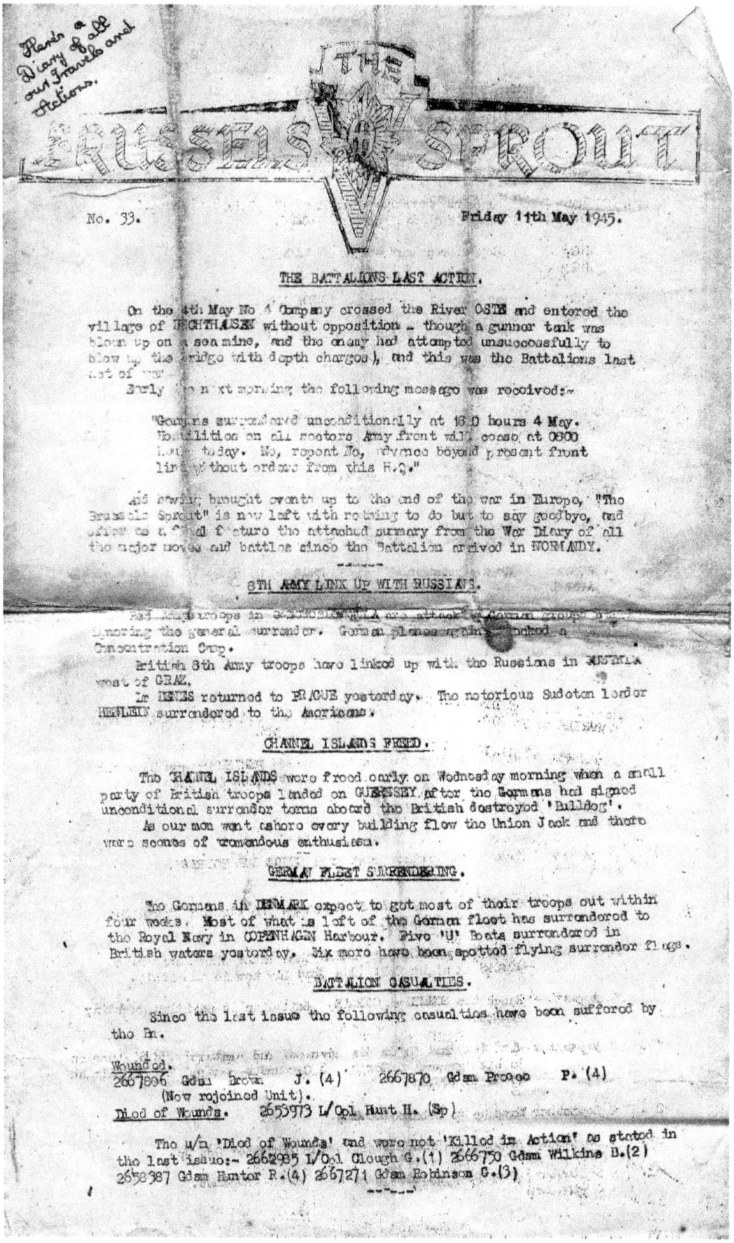

Here's a
Diary of all
our Travels and
Actions.

THE BRUSSELS SPROUT

No. 33. Friday 11th May 1945.

THE BATTALIONS LAST ACTION.

On the 4th May No 4 Company crossed the River OSTE and entered the village of HECHTHAUSEN without opposition - though a gunner tank was blown up on a sea mine, and the enemy had attempted unsuccessfully to blow up the bridge with depth charges), and this was the Battalions last act of war.

Early [illegible] next morning the following message was received:-

"Germans surrendered unconditionally at 1820 hours 4 May. Hostilities on all sectors Army front will cease at 0800 hours today. No, repeat No, advance beyond present front line without orders from this H.Q."

And having brought events up to the end of the war in Europe, "The Brussels Sprout" is now left with nothing to do but to say goodbye, and offer as a final feature the attached summary from the War Diary of all the major moves and battles since the Battalion arrived in NORMANDY.

8TH ARMY LINK UP WITH RUSSIANS.

Red Army troops in [illegible] are attacking German groups [illegible] ignoring the general surrender. German planes again attacked a Concentration Camp.

British 8th Army troops have linked up with the Russians in AUSTRIA west of GRAZ.

Dr BENES returned to PRAGUE yesterday. The notorious Sudeten leader HENLEIN surrendered to the Americans.

CHANNEL ISLANDS FREED.

The CHANNEL ISLANDS were freed early on Wednesday morning when a small party of British troops landed on GUERNSEY after the Germans had signed unconditional surrender terms aboard the British destroyed 'Bulldog'.

As our men went ashore every building flew the Union Jack and there were scenes of tremendous enthusiasm.

GERMAN FLEET SURRENDERING.

The Germans in DENMARK expect to get most of their troops out within four weeks. Most of what is left of the German fleet has surrendered to the Royal Navy in COPENHAGEN Harbour. Five 'U' Boats surrendered in British waters yesterday. Six more have been spotted flying surrender flags.

BATTALION CASUALTIES.

Since the last issue the following casualties have been suffered by the Bn.

Wounded.
2667806 Gdsm Brown J. (4) 2667870 Gdsm Proceo P. (4)
(Now rejoined Unit).
Died of Wounds. 2653973 L/Cpl Hunt H. (Sp)

The u/m 'Died of Wounds' and were not 'Killed in Action' as stated in the last issue:- 2662985 L/Cpl Clough G.(1) 2666750 Gdsm Wilkins B.(2) 2658387 Gdsm Hunter R.(4) 2667271 Gdsm Robinson G.(3)

The Brussels Sprout front cover with Grandad's writing in the top left corner;
'Here's a diary of all our travels and actions.'

Above: A 20 Franc coin dated 1933, from Steve's war time collection of artefacts.

Above: 50 Franc bank note dated 1944, another souvenir from France during the war years.

Norman Bryant taken from larger photo of 13th Coy 1941 see page 22.

WEST YORKSHIRE

Facing Page: This old battered Toffee Tin held a small treasure trove of his artefacts; West Yorkshire Regiment Cap Badge (Silver Horse), an Italian Prize Pendant for rifle shooting, 2 x small Coldstream Regimental Button, a larger Royal Artillery Regiment Tunic Button 2 x Officers Collar Cuffs a Coldstream Guards Cap Star and a French Pin Badge which reads On Ne Passes Pas, translated They Shall Not Pass.

Above: Coldstream Guards Regimental Buttons from Steve's Toffee Tin collection of artefacts.

Right: A West Yorkshire Regiment Cap Badge from Steve's collection.

Above: A Coldstream Guards Regiment Officers Cap Badge
from his collection.

Below: These are two Officers Insignia collar cuffs
from Steve's collection.

This is the French pin badge reading, 'On ne passé pas.' translated, 'They shall not pass.' It is a slogan used by the French after WWI and during WWII expressing their determination they would defend their positions and the enemy would not pass. After WWI France was determined they should never suffer appalling damage again to their men, people and buildings, they created The Maginot Line spreading along the French/German border, it was a series of outposts dominated by large forts, built to defend France from another German invasion named after their War Minister.
www.historylearningsite.co.uk

3

'HE'D NOT EVEN SEEN A GERMAN!'

· On July 11th the unit was pulled back to St Martin-les-Entrees for a rest period in preparation for Operation Goodwood, the complete liberation of the city of Caen. **History of the 5th Bn Coldstream Guards www.5thbncoldstreamguards.com**

Well there'd been such a demand for reinforcements I was fortunate compared to a lot of young men as I had a long time at training and had the experience over a lot of young men, I ended up teaching some y'know I got to so I could teach my knowledge and I couldn't have been, nobody could have been better prepared to go into action than I was y'see, I mean there were a lot of young men green, green as grass were a lot and had a few months training, then they came out to you y'know. It was a sad part, in fact we were under attack once and I was having to demonstrate to some young lads how to prime a grenade and get the grenade ready for some use, I mean an attack were coming in y'know and that were a thing I were there having to do like.

It was a killer in the trenches particularly if you were on a front which was very active with a lot of shelling and mortaring , or you'd done an attack and were dug in, you'd be two hours on, two hours off and at first light just as the light was breaking, they use to call it 'Stand To' everybody for an hour, everybody, cook, and bottle washers the lot were stood up in their trench with their arms at the ready until it came daylight, sometimes it was so hard to keep your eyes open, you could fall asleep standing up like, but if you were caught asleep it was severe punishment, that was the hard one, trying to keep awake y'know. I remember another old pal of mine Tommy Witon, he's dead now poor old Tom, we'd pulled back into Battalion area from our patrol and I was laid in my trench, couldn't sleep like, they were shelling all around us and I could hear guitar music, y'know Hawaiian guitar music, I could hear it in my head so I said to Tommy,

'Do you know Tom, I've been laid in my trench 'ere and all I could hear was bloody Hawaiian guitar music.' he said,

'Do you know Stephen I was the same, I could hear bloody music there too.'

To put it bluntly you were scared you were frightened y'know, in my case and I suppose in lots of them, you thought 'Well I don't want to let my mates see I'm a coward' but I was, I was frightened to death y'know, I think if anyone says he wasn't he's definitely telling porky's, I went through it all and the things

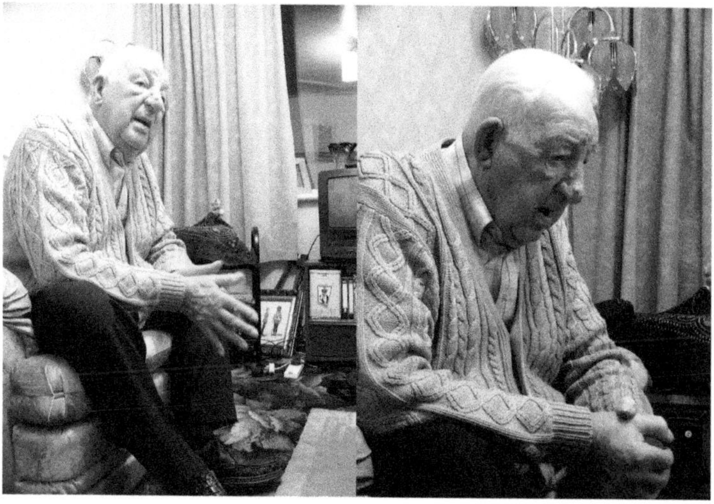

I did y'know, I was absolutely shit scared but I did it, I knew if I didn't do it they would think I'm a yellow bastard y'know, you needed strength or you had to have something y'know like, the old woodbine and a sip of whiskey were good aids, and as I say you'd have some good mates, you could have a giggle y'know, have a laugh at something silly, it kept you going.

As I say there'd been such a demand for reinforcements and what not y'know like, I recall a very sad occasion it were upsetting, we'd been, I forget the name of the place exactly but it was in Normandy, we'd advanced so far and then we reached a valley like, then it was like an escarpment y'know you'd to climb up the sides, well there'd been 1 or 2 Regiment's who had had a go up here and they'd been knocked back, well of course the old 5th Battalion, bloody nutters, they sent them in and we managed it, but we were followed through by the Carriers and there were this 'ere lad at the side of the road, he had come up as reinforcements at night time y'see, it were very sad, he were just quivering and he'd just had it like, it was so sad he's just laid at the side of the road and bloody dusts covering all over him and what not y'know, that was an upsetting thing. So as I say poor buggar he'd not even seen a German y'know, he was just taken from his home and 'pppsh FINITO!' Like I say I was lucky, well I think right through my service luck were with me.

'At this point in the interview my Grandad just broke down and started to cry for the young boy he had seen. It took a long pause before he continued with his interview.'

So then we had some devastating news, my pal Bill Wigglesworth, took a patrol out onto the area of the Carpiquet Aerodrome, the lads dismounted and the three drivers were left with the vehicles, well whilst they were out they must have been spotted and the Germans put a barrage down on the vehicles and the three lads were killed (Bill survived) but there was a lad called George Cobby, we'd been together right from our first day of service, we were in the same squad and had soldiered right together like, then there was a boy from Leeds called Tom Dean and another young man, young married man called Tommy Johnson, they were all killed together, they're now buried side by side in St Mauvieux Cemetery which I visited three times like, y'know.

'Amongst Grandad's artefacts are copies of three certificates which commemorate the Guardsmen he speaks of here, George R Cobby age 21, Thomas Dean age 19 and Thomas Johnson age 22 died 29th June 1944 see Fig. 42- Fig.47.'

I intend going again on the 60th anniversary on D-Day, which is the 6th June 2004, like I say anyway, our officer came up, Captain Fanning came and told us the news we were all really cut up, it wasn't the first time we had lost casualties, no we had lost some lads the night that we went into the line, they were coming up as reinforcements, as they were coming up they were shelled on their way in and a lad called Les Ascough he was badly wounded and died of his wounds, an old mate of mine Neddy Hunt, he was very badly wounded but he survived like y'know but he was left badly crippled for life through it all, I've seen him twice since he was wounded and he's still the same old Ned y'know.

'Grandad chuckles to himself and remembers Ned with great fondness.'

From then we took a lot of shelling in our positions eventually when our armour landed in France they brought us out of the line for a rest period, our nerves were on end and we were all very jumpy for quite a number of days, they say smoking's bad for you but did we give the bloody cigarettes some stick y'know, some of the lads they'd discovered the local drink in some of the battered farm houses it was a very potent drink called Calvados, they all had their water bottles filled with it to steady their nerves like y'see. (When I was younger I always had the thought that my Mum was watching over me and that nothing would get me, I think that was what had helped me get through, apart from cigarettes and a good stiff drink.)

- Brussels Sprout read action No. 3 11th to 17th July 1944: Back in rest area of Bayeux.
  Brussels Sprout Diary

Bottom left corner is George Cobby, this is part of the photograph taken of 13th Coy Sergeant Browns training squad back in England in 1941, stood by his side is Billy Wigglesworth. For full photograph see page 22.

In Memory of
Lance Corporal GEORGE R. COBBY

2664221, 5th Bn., Coldstream Guards
who died age 21
on 29 June 1944
Son of Walter and Ada Cobby, of Hull.

Remembered with honour
ST. MANVIEU WAR CEMETERY, CHEUX

Commemorated in perpetuity by
the Commonwealth War Graves Commission

From Steve's collection, the commemorative certificate for George Cobby, killed during their very first engagement of war.

This is one of Steve's photographs taken from his album, George Cobby's grave stone St Mauvieux Cemetery in France, he was only 21, Steve had known him since the first day of joining up.

Thomas Dean's grave stone, one of Steve's own photographs from his album.

In Memory of
Guardsman THOMAS DEAN

2665611, 5th Bn., Coldstream Guards
who died age 19
on 29 June 1944
Son of Richard and Hilda Dean, of Leeds, Yorkshire.

Remembered with honour
ST. MANVIEU WAR CEMETERY, CHEUX

Commemorated in perpetuity by
the Commonwealth War Graves Commission

Gdsm Thomas Dean commemorative certificate, killed age 19 years old, a teenager!

In Memory of
Guardsman THOMAS JOHNSON

2661135, 6th Bn., Coldstream Guards
who died age 24
on 29 June 1944
Son of Thomas and Selina Johnson, of Leeds,
Yorkshire; husband of Doris Johnson, of Leeds.

Remembered with honour
ST. MANVIEU WAR CEMETERY, CHEUX

Commemorated in perpetuity by
the Commonwealth War Graves Commission

Left: Thomas Johnson's commemorative certificate. Right: Thomas Johnson's grave stone, one of Steve's own photographs from his album, this man was only 24 when he was killed in action, he was also married.

Taken during a rest and refitting period Carpiquet Aerodrome area 1944. It looks warm so I put this circa July 1944.
Reg Baker, Tommy Musgrove, Unknown, Marsh Eggleston, Stephen Simpson, Peacock, Unknown, Unkown, Ollie, Unkown, Unknown, Charlie Coverdale

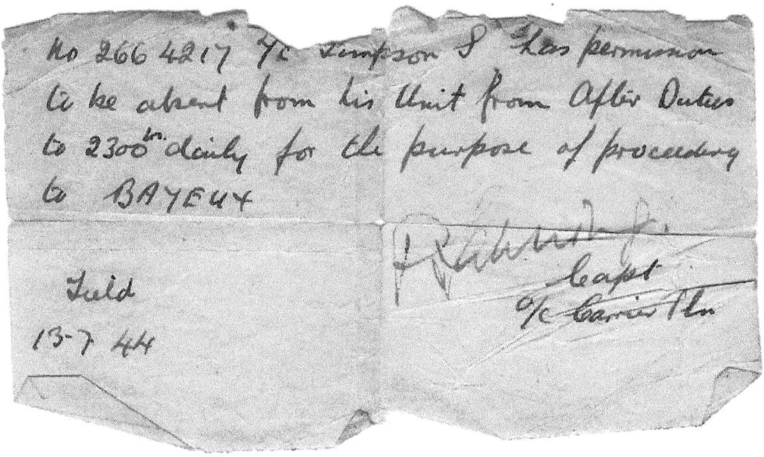
No 2664217 Pte Simpson S has permission to be absent from his Unit from After Duties to 2300hrs daily for the purpose of proceeding to BAYEUX

Field
13-7 44

Capt
O/c Carrier Pln

A small scrap of paper found amongst Steve's artefacts
representing a pass out, it reads:
"No. 2664217 Simpson S has permission to be about from his unit from after duties to 2300hrs daily for the purpose of proceeding to Bayeux. Dated 13.07.44"

This birthday card was posted to Beryl on her 16th birthday, it was with all the collection the box it was in has a handwritten note 'From Steve on my 16th Birthday 7th July 1944.' It is very touching that he was engaging in his first battles, losing his good friends and still found the effort to not forget her birthday, source a card and post it.

4

'THE ONE THAT WAS TAKING THE BRUNT.'

- Brussels Sprout read action No. 4 18th July 1944:
  Took part in Operation Goodwood to enlarge the bridge head in front of newly captured Caen. Battalion took over position in area of Cagny from armed brigade.
  Brussels Sprout Diary

Eventually we joined up with the armour and on the 18th July the three Armoured Divisions went into action, we crossed over the Pegasus Bridge which the Airborne had taken on D-Day itself, that was an amazing feat and to see where the gliders had landed right amongst the German positions y'know, and stormed the bridge and taken the bridge and held it against everything the Germans could throw at them like. As I say we crossed over on the morning of the 18th July, prior to us going over a thousand Bomber planes came in and bombed three villages on the way into our objective, the idea was that it would knock the enemy out but unfortunately they suffered a lot of casualties but the majority of them had got out of the villages already. While we were in active service and going into a village and seeing a persons home shattered and their belongings slung about it really got you for the first few times, but then of course you get case hardened, it's like seeing a soldier dead, your thoughts are,

'Oh someone's got some sadness here'

And then later on it's just another dead body that's just how your feelings were, I don't say you were insensitive but if you didn't get it out of your system like that you'd dwell on it and you'd be no good y'know. When we started advancing they were back in the villages and it was terrific fighting just to get the villages cleared, they'd also got lines of Anti Tank Guns and the Tanks, there was three divisions of tanks and I forget how many tanks there was in a division, but they had half of the tanks knocked out in action on that particular day. We did make an advance but it was against very, very hard opposition and shelling both from Artillery and from the Anti Tank Guns, it was very hair raising and very frightening. Eventually we captured a place called Cagny, there we dug in and we were subjected to a lot of artillery fire, after about 4 or 5 days we were relieved by an Infantry Regiment I think it was a Scots Regiment.

They took over from us, we'd to leave all our Anti Tank Guns in position because there had been terrific amounts of rain and we couldn't pull the guns out of the earth y'see, so we left our guns in and took the guns of the people relieving us.

- Brussels Sprout No. 6 23rd July - 28th July 1944:
  Semi rest area at Giberville. Decoy to German Panzer Division and at notice to take part in advance towards Brettiville Sur Laize. Guards Armoured Division part cancelled.
  Brussels Sprout Diary No.33.

- The battalion manoeuvred with the division going through Couverville and Demouville before meeting the 12th SS with heavy fighting at Frenouville before being pulled back to Giberville, again for a rest period. A month into its Normandy campaign the battalion had suffered 200 casualties, killed and wounded.

So we pulled back onto a ridge and we were there, it turned out that we were acting as a decoy because the Germans brought all their strength an armour around onto our front. We were subjected to a lot of Anti Tank fire and we were bombed at night time as well, the idea was that we were in this decoy position and it turned out the Americans on the sections on the opposite side to where we were, well they broke through then, so then all the armour was on our front so we had a lot of hard fighting but we did break through.

Then I was taken ill, I had a very bad dose of tonsillitis my Officer told me to go sick. I reported to our Regimental Aid Post and I was despatched to the General Hospital near Bayeux, I was there for a weekend and in the mean time our division had started their defensive at a place called St Martin.

- Brussels Sprout No.8 31st July 1944:
  Took up advance of Guards Armoured Division with tanks of 2nd Irish from St Martin to pt 204.
  Brussels Sprout Diary

I remember an incident, old Jack, I remind him of it, when I came out of hospital the Division had been battling at the top of this here hill, they had gotten cut off and they thought they would have cleared it but the 15th Scottish Division had had to come round and clear the way so you could get to back to them, I come back outta hospital and went to report to my Platoon Officer Captain Fanning, as I say they were all dug in like they had been bombed and shelled and what not for a time, so this 'ere bloody blackened face pops up from a trench.

'Eh up Simmy are ya alright? Bloody tiger tanks were round here.'

And down he goes again and it were old Jack. We'd very hard battles, our battalions always seemed to be the one that was taking the brunt y'know, and I don't know whether I'm right in thinking that but it always seemed to be us that had the very hard fighting.

'At this point in the interview my Grandad's voice broke badly and he got very upset. He paused a while to regain some composure'.

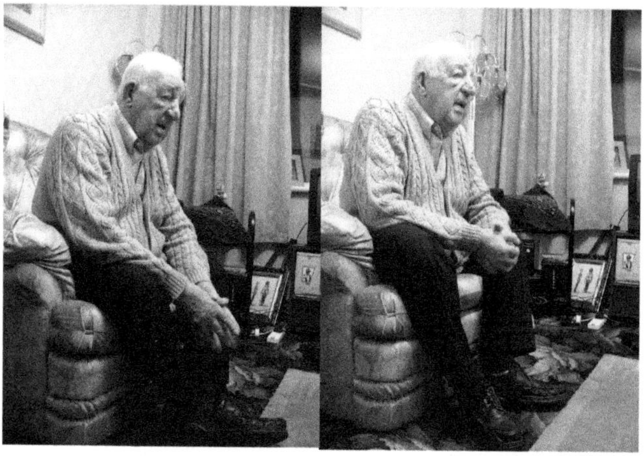

- The next stages of the fighting were towards Falaise with consistent engagements against SS troops at Caumont, St Martin Des Besuces and St Charles De Percy, leading to a large battle at La Marvindiere, where they were, for a time, surrounded by mechanised German infantry and armour, taking 300 casualties but repelling determined German attacks and holding their ground. From here the unit was pulled back to a quieter part of the line until the end of the Falaise pocket battles, by which time the 5th was moved to Chenedolle for a badly needed rest and reorganisation, during which time, due to the depletion of the battle companies, the 5th Battalion was reduced from 4 battle companies to 3.

History of the 5th Bn Coldstream Guards www.5thbncoldstreamguards.com

- Brussels Sprout No.9 1st August – 5th August 1944:
  Advance continued via St Charles De Percy to Lamarvindiere.
  Brussels Sprout Diary

There was quite a number of very, very heavy people casualties sometimes but we kept going, eventually we'd move through places some places come to mind we'd St Charles De Percy, Lebusq, eventually the ring tightened on the Germans, the Canadians were pushing from the left and the Polish Army. The days of 1944 from June till August vicious battles took part in Normandy, eventually after the closure of the Falaise Pocket where the majority of the German Army was seen off, it was only speckles of like the SS which escaped across the river.

- Brussels Sprout No.13 12th August – 16th August 1944:
  Withdrawn back to position by Bas Feriere: from here the enemy withdrew from us via the Falaise Pocket.
  Brussels Sprout Diary

The Americans were on the right and we were in the centre, we closed the gap at Falaise it was very, very strong fighting, the Germans were trapped and the Typhoons and the Bombers went inland, they really devastated, nearly wiped out the German forces, some of them did manage to escape.

Now then finally it was the River Seine, we cleared it and all the areas were cleared in Normandy then. So for a week we had rest and recuperation, then we moved from a place called Flers after refitting and the Americans broke round on the right and made for Paris. We went through Northern France and after the desolation and battering that we'd seen in Normandy just to get out into nice country and pass through villages that weren't damaged y' know and be greeted as liberators by people was lovely. We crossed a bridge that the engineers had built, we crossed over and from then on we kept meeting with light opposition but we battled on and we got through to the Somme.

- Brussels Sprout No.18 31st:
  August Reach the Somme at Corble. Battalion in position guarding bridges.
  Brussels Sprout Diary

- The 5th battalion then moved to rejoin the division moving up to the Somme on defensive operations which mainly involved the rounding up of German prisoners. The 5th battalion then combined into a battle formation with the 1st battalion Coldstream Guards which was one of the armoured battalions of the Guards Armoured Division. This combination of infantry and armour battalions was a common formation employed by the division for the rest of the war. Using this formation Arras was taken without a major conflict, with German resistance being quickly overcome.
  History of the 5th Bn Coldstream Guards www.5thbncoldstreamguards.com

We held the river there for a day and a night and then we crossed the Somme across to Arras and the town itself for a few days, then the orders came in we were to move on, we were to attack Arras and take Arras, when we were crossing the Somme it was heart breaking to see the vast areas of graves from the First World War, you could look up over this ridge and there were thousands of gravestones y'know, a big cemetery like and it made you think. Eventually we had a bit of a tussle and we managed to take Arras, we took part in the liberation of Arras and from there we moved on then to Douai and Tournai, people were absolutely crazy meeting us like, once we consolidated we moved through Arras to a ridge outside the town ready to go onto our next objective. While we were there harboured, three spitfires came over and startled us, they set fire to the petrol wagon and the ammunition truck which went up in flames. They didn't expect us to be so far forward and they thought it was the Germans, anyway that was another little incident of so-called friendly fire, and fortunately there were no casualties.

Funny little incident happened Bill Wigglesworth and I, we got into Arras and most us of were suffering with diarrhoea and dysentery what with all the flies on your food and what not, we had what we called a 14-man pack; it had rations for the day for 14 men, it had 5 cigs each, 3 sheets of toilet paper, a tin of biscuits, bully beef, sardines or salmon, soup, steam pudding or rice pudding y'know, you'd have a variety of different packs y'see and what they used to do for a latrine if you were in a dug in position, was cut the hole in the box for a seat with a lid on y'see. Well you'd lift the lid up and you'd sit on it and you'd nearly lift up with bloody flies y'know, there were millions off of dead bodies and what not, so most of us contracted dysentery, one incident, old Horace he bails out, convoy had stopped so he grabs a shovel and he's away over fields, but he came back,

'Oh it was too late!' he said and had taken his trousers off.

Anyway one building as we got into Arras, there was this here bombed building and me and old Bill we were taken short so we nipped in, trousers whipped down, we turned round and did our business, it turned out there was a bloody audience.

- Brussels Sprout No.21 3rd September 1944:
  Advance to Brussels following Grenedier Gds Gp.
  Brussels Sprout Diary

From then we moved on to a place called Roubaix we had a couple of days refitting and then came the big break through to Brussels which was on September 3rd.

Orders came through that we were going to advance on Brussels it was 90 miles away, it was quite a tall order but we set off early morning and we did get to Brussels, it was the longest march and fastest march in history that had been accomplished that day by the Guards Armoured Division, fastest and longest advance British Army had ever made to Brussels, Bren Carriers, Tanks the lot y'know, the Infantry Carriers, we were Lorried Infantry y'see, TCL Troop Carriers. We fought our way through opposition here and there at different places, we met pockets of resistance but if it was really difficult we had to bypass and go around it as we were to press on to Brussels. Where we by-passed them the Infantry Division which was following us took care of them, they would clear the places of the Germans. Eventually the evening of September 3rd we just got to the outskirts of Brussels, just as dusk was falling but we were stopped for no reason we thought, the people there were absolutely ecstatic, they were wild we were absolutely mobbed by people on the outskirts, eventually we received orders to go into Brussels itself and take over the city, we were held back and it turned out the reason why we'd been held there was a Belgium Brigade at the rear of us was supposed to be coming in to take the honour of liberating the city, well we'd gone that fast and got there so quick that they were miles back, so we had to go in to take the city there and then in case the Germans started trying to return back y'see.

'Amongst Grandad's collection of memorabilia was an old booklet, an original from The Guards Armoured Division. Farewell To Armour Parade. Rotenburg Airfield, Germany 9th June 1945.

Field Marshal Montgomery addressed the division as they were been disbanded as they were no longer needed due to the surrender of the Germans, this is a quote from his speech';

'After prolonged training on Salisbury Plain, in Norfolk, and on the Yorkshire Wolds, the Guards Armoured Division landed in France last June and it had two months of hard fighting in the Normandy bridge head. The division then crossed the river Seine and took part in the sensational advance through Belgium into Holland, completing then the most rapid advance of a division in history – from Douiai to Brussels, 97 miles, in 14 hours.'

Field Marshal Montgomery Farewell To Armour Parade

(For the complete speech see Chapter Seven.)

Above: Sienne

Below: German Prisoners

Below: German convoy

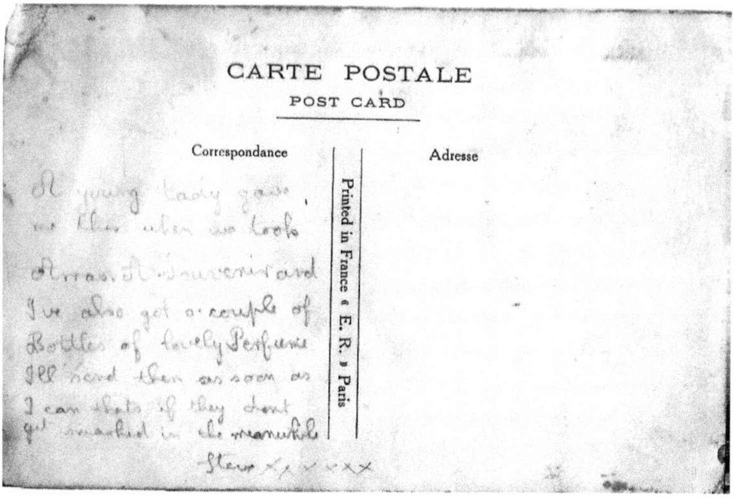

Postcard posted back to Beryl circa
August / September 1944 on the back it reads;

'A young lady gave me this when we took Arras. A souvenir and I've also got a couple of bottles of lovely perfume, I'll send them as soon as I can, that's if they don't get smashed in the meanwhile.
Steve xxxxx'

This is a post card Steve from Brussels, on the back Steve has written;

'This is a view of the Royal Palace. I saw it when we entered Brussels in September and it sure is a lovely place but for that matter the whole city is grand and my only regret is that I didn't see more of it when we passed through.'

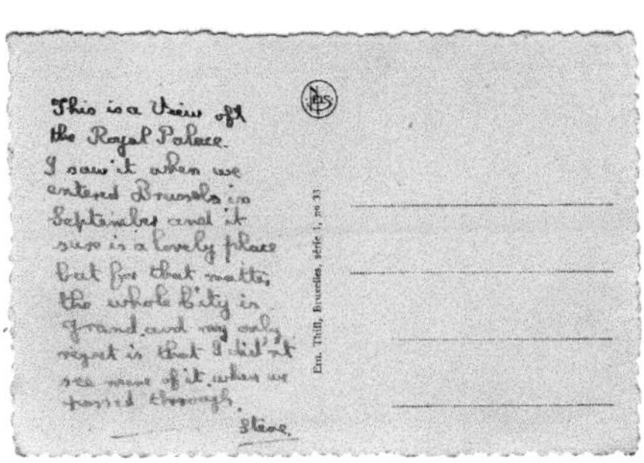

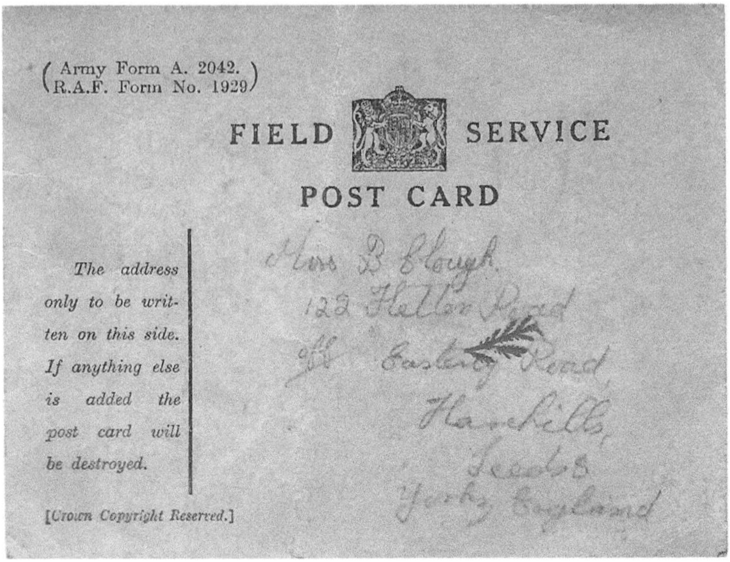

(Army Form A. 2042.
R.A.F. Form No. 1929)

FIELD SERVICE

POST CARD

The address only to be written on this side. If anything else is added the post card will be destroyed.

Mrs B Clough
122 Hetton Road
Off Easterly Road
Harehills,
Leeds 8
Yorks England

[*Crown Copyright Reserved.*]

This is an original Field Postcard dated 1st September 1944, addressed to Beryl, amongst Steve's collection. It is a standard post card on the reverse are multiple choice statements that the field soldier crossed off where relevant, no other information was given in case they were intercepted and could hinder the war effort. In this post card he has highlighted 'I am quite well.'

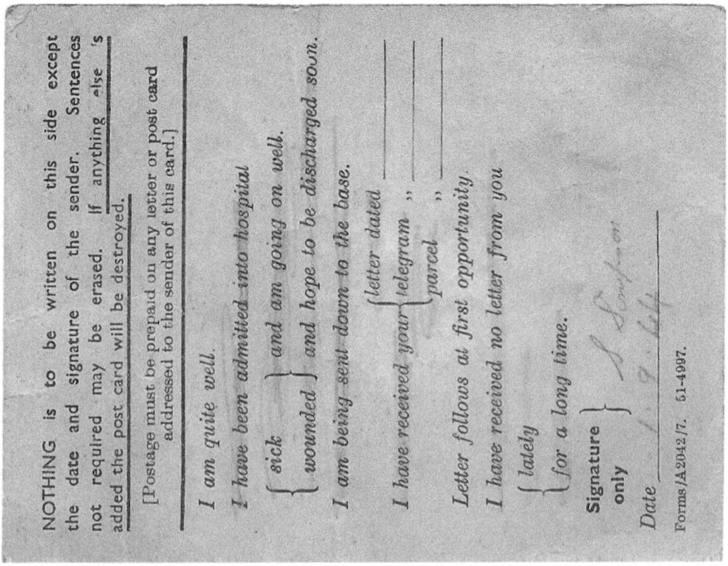

NOTHING is to be written on this side except the date and signature of the sender. Sentences not required may be erased. If anything else is added the post card will be destroyed.

[Postage must be prepaid on any letter or post card addressed to the sender of this card.]

I am quite well.

I have been admitted into hospital

{sick} and am going on well.

{wounded} and hope to be discharged soon.

I am being sent down to the base.

I have received your {letter dated / telegram " / parcel "}

Letter follows at first opportunity.

I have received no letter from you {lately / for a long time.}

Signature only

Date

Forms/A2042/7. 51-4997.

A 50 Cent Belgium Coin dated 1923 from Steve's collection.

This is a Belgium 20 Franc note and the design was early 1940, it wasn't changed under the German occupation and still depicts King Albert and Queen Elisabeth paper notes were issued by the army. This original was among Steve's collection.

Citizens of Brussels immediately after the liberation.

5

'THE ROYAL ROYAL'S'

I have never seen anything like it in my life, the population were out lining the streets and they were absolutely ecstatic were the folks, what a thrill that was y'know to have taken part in such an event.

'Grandad's voice started to break again as he filled with emotion at the memory of the people and their happiness at been liberated after 4 years of German occupation.'

You'd have thought we were the Royal Royals, every human body was swarming all over us like, they threw flowers and rode jumping on your tanks and carriers, absolutely wild it was, so we pulled into the square in Brussels and a funny thing happened. Our captain Fanning, Percy Fanning a smashing little fella wasn't particularly tall y'know, he had big rosy cheeks y'know and this here woman got a hold of him and she was kissing him, she was well pregnant y'know and so we were all going,

'Come on Percy, go on Percy'

'Madame, Madame' he's saying y'know flapping his arms around all embarrassed like but we laughed.

Then we were found billets in a big hotel you could never imagine the luxury we felt from sitting on a toilet seat y'know, oh after squatting over a pit on a bar or on a ration box to sit down on the seat of a toilet was absolute luxury y'know. I must of been sat there two hours it was beautiful, as I say just a little thing like that oh how you appreciated it. Because previously dug in, in position we'd have a latrine dug and you'd sit on a box in a most uncomfortable way of doing your business because the flies, there were millions of flies and one thing I must remember particularly in Normandy was the smell of cattle and horse that had been killed. It was absolutely horrendous was the smell and of course of decomposing bodies you see. Oh that's a memory that still smells.

'During our trip to Regimental HQ I was able to take away the following account written by Captain Ian Oswald Liddell V.C of the 5th Battalion. This is a fantastic account of the liberation the 5th Battalion took part in through Arras and onto Brussels, my Grandad shared this experience with Captain Liddell all the way, yet Ian Liddell really captures the joyous heartfelt experience the liberators received from the people in full;'

156048 Capt. I.O. Liddell,
5th Battalion Coldstream Guards,
B.L.A
8.9.1944

Dear Jim,

As the wireless has just announced the achievement of the Guards Armoured Division in the last few days, it is permissible to write a personal account, and I thought it might interest you so I enclose a copy of the one I have sent home.

They have been very great days. At last we have had a real job to show our merit which has been a very pleasant change after having had all the foulest jobs of the campaign to date, at Caens, Vire, Mortaigne and

Falaise. As you will see from the account it has been pretty hectic and we are not finished yet.

As our latest exploits have been announced on the wireless it is now O.K. for us to write about it, so herewith one of my "news letters".

We started off with a 100 miles approach march to the Seine which we crossed at Vernon. The officer in charge of the bridge there was of all people Tom Evill who looked very well and was very cheerful having built the bridge the day before in record time under fire.

We moved straight to the Somme which we crossed at Amiens. The reception we got once we crossed the Seine was wonderful. Cheering crowds the whole way – every vehicle covered with flowers, every man covered with lipstick, and everyone full of fruit.

From Amiens we made a dash for Arras which was very exciting as we just went flat out and bypassed pockets of resistance, leaving them to the F.F.I. who were the most desperate looking band of brigands I have ever seen but wonderfully efficient. We were able to hand all our prisoners over to them and leave all the small pockets of enemy for them to deal with. They were worth several divisions to us for guarding our lines of communication.

Then we arrived at Arras. An armoured group consisting of our 1st Bn. In tanks with ourselves as infantry were the first to enter. I went in on my motorcycle with the leading troop of tanks. Such was the speed of our advance that we caught the Germans napping and then began what was the most amazing and fantastically unreal experience of my life. As we entered the town a few cautious heads were poked out of windows and then with a roar everyone surged out into the roads and swarmed all over our vehicles. At that moment about 20 Germans ran out of an alleyway and started running down the road. Our tanks simpy could not fire because there were so many civilians all over the vehicles and roads. Then began the most fantastic part of it all because I rode up and down the road in amongst them all – Germans included – shouting to the civilians over my amplifier for the civilians to get off the roads. This they did with amazing alacrity once they realized the position, and very cunningly locked their doors so that when the Germans tried to run across from one house to another they found the doors barred. I had great fun with a band of the Patriots going down the back of a row of houses and throwing smoke grenades into the windows which bolted the Boche most successfully, but I am afraid did the houses no good. If they bolted out of the front the tanks got them, and if they came out of the back, we did. After half an hour of this they started surrendering and in no time we had several hundred.

The people by this time were in a frenzy of excitement and lined the streets ten deep screaming at the top of their voices and giving us everything from bottles of beer and wine to live pigs!

From here we made another dash, this time to Brussels. You can gather from my description that the French gave us a very good reception but what the Belgians gave us I am incapable of describing. All I can say is that I have never seen or imagined such heartfelt joy and thankfulness as the Belgians showed. Just to show you what I mean, they sang the British National Anthem for 65 minutes outside the Palace of Justice which is their most treasured and historical building in Brussels, and which the Germans wantonly set fire to as we entered the city, and which was still blazing fiercely.

We arrived just before dark and drove straight to the centre of the city. Our route was lined with thousands of delirious people with torches, who screamed at every vehicle that went past.

Without exaggeration at all I can truthfully say that I was nearer killed by the joy of the people in Brussels than I have been since we landed. I stopped on a crossroads to see the column pass and the crowd rushed at me. The main idea seemed to merely to touch me but in doing so the crowd surged across the road blocking the route completely, dragged me off my machine, smacked me on the back, kissed me, and in general very nearly knocked me unconscious. We could not sleep a wink that night although we had only 5 hours sleep in the previous four days because we were guarding our vehicles and weapons from souvenir hunters. I know this all sounds fantastic and wildly exaggerated but it is not.

Next day it was unsafe to enter Brussels unless in a vehicle with doors you could lock, and with windows up, otherwise you were rushed at by men and women alike who kissed you, buffeted you, screamed at you, and wept on you. All Brussels was "En Fete". In the afternoon I was driving through the town when two newspaper correspondents, whom I had got to know well in those last few days (Edwards who writes for News Chronicle and Chester Wilmott the broadcaster), shouted at me to come and have some tea with them. We very unwisely entered the biggest cafe in the place. No sooner had we entered the room than everyone stood up and cheered for about 2 minutes. We were then dragged up to the front table and thought we would get something to eat. But not a bit of it. The band stood up, the customers stood up, and we sang the National Anthem, the Belgian National

Anthem, the Marseillaise, and the Star Spangled Banner. After that we thought –TEA But no. We were dragged on to the stage (Thunderous applause) and made to sing Tipperary through the microphone. That of course was too much of a good thing and everyone screamed themselves hoarse with applause. Then Monsieur le Patron made a speech of which we could not understand a word as it was in Flemish and then each of us had to make a speech – a speech which I am equally sure they did not understand a word, and then Monsieur le Patron kissed us on both cheeks with tears rolling down his cheeks. All very embarrassing and we got no tea!

In between this we had been mopping up the City and got quite a good bag. One of the best things was that we got there so quickly that the Boche did not have time to take away all the political prisoners he had in jail.

I had my photograph taken in hundreds of admiring groups and gave my home address to all of them who promised to write to me forever and ever send me all the photos, so you may see some photographs of me yet!

You'll have heard the figures of our advance on the wireless. 400 miles in 9 days with one stretch of 260 miles in 4 days. Our exhaustion is very great but we are all in terrific form, and although we have come very quickly we have been able to inflict heavy casualties on the Boche. I may say we have not finished yet.

The transport is standing up to it wonderfully. We have to improvise all the time. We have found that champagne corks make very good plugs for bullet holes in petrol tanks, and having been given 800 magnums of champagne in Brussels we have plentiful supply of corks!

We are still hard at it so I must stop now. You'll be hearing of us again doing big things.

Much love

Ian.

'The poignancy of this letter is such that it was the last letter Capt. Ian Oswald Liddell wrote home. He did continue to do 'big things', a short while after this letter was written he single handily disarmed a bridge whilst under fire, more of which is mentioned in Chapter Seven, for this great act of selfless bravery he was awarded the Victoria Cross.'

- The division then turned towards Belgium, liberating Brussels before crossing the Albert and Escaut canals. The 5th was involved in heavy fighting in Rovelle during the canal crossing, moving on to Beverloo during the battle and moving in to secure a bridge head over the Escaut. By this time the battalion had been reduced to 3 weak companies and was pulled back to La Colonie in preparation for transfer to Linden for Operation Market Garden in Holland.

  History of the 5th Bn Coldstream Guards
  www.5thbncoldstreamguards.com

The morning after the liberation my platoon was detailed off to go out onto a patrol through the other side of the city, we did eventually, once we were all fully supplied again and we started to advance to a place called Albert then onto a place called Hasalt, where the most severe fighting happened.

When you tried to dig in on the hills there was very little protection and you'd try to dig in to only get down a foot, it was very sandy and wet, a certain thing happened; we all wanted a blighty, a little wound in your backside or a pitted arm so you could get back out like y'see, one, old George Hardy use to lay in a trench with his leg sticking up and out like hoping he'd get bloody shrapnel, huh he got his shrapnel but it got him in the back and it were a really, really bad wound for George.

Arthur Davis he were the same, oh he got his blighty, he'd been in Dunkirk and he'd just had it, a bloody shell landed miles away from us he got perforated eardrums and off he went.

'Oh' he says 'Hear that I'm off.'

From there we fought on and suffered a lot of casualties again, in fact one company was nearly decimated.

'The memory at the huge losses overcame my Grandad at this stage in the interview and his voice started to break, he reflected for a moment.'

- Brussels Sprout No.24 & 25 8th September – 10th September 1944:
  By expanding bridgehead from Beringen: fought battles Beverloo and Heppen just west of Bourg Leopold.
  Brussels Sprout Diary

As my memory takes me, we moved on to a place called Bourg Leopold where we fought to clear that area, this had been a training area for the German Army, a big camp there, we took the barracks and the training area, then we moved to what they call the Escaut Canal, which was just before the border from Holland. It was at the Escaut Canal that we had some vicious fighting on rainy nights, I recall a German attacker a company's strength came in over the canal we could see them and the Cromwell Tanks they came in and we sorted them out like.

I recall an incident happened here, my lot we used to collect all sorts of weapons and guns like, when we were driving about, my Captain once said,

'Simpson, your Carrier looks like a Tinkers workshop!' to which I replied,

'Thank you Sir.'

Well we'd got this here German Spandau and we got it fitted up and we were dug in at the edge of this hedge and we opened up with this Spandau. Well one of these Tanks started to turn around, because they had a sound of their own did theses Spandau's y'see, so it's turning around and he comes up on us ready to shoot, we jumped up waving are arms around saying,

'No. No. No', they thought it were Germans y'see, so we said,

'Right were getting rid of that bloody thing quick smart like'

It was a real rapid fire machine gun, so we got rid of that.

We crossed and I think the place was a coal mining area; we had a lot of casualties some very fierce fighting y'know, the Anti-tank lads had had a birthday, they knocked two tanks out down this here road, we held there and the plans were in progress for the Air Drop in Arnhem y'see. At the canal we were there about a week because the armour was so badly damaged they were refitting and we were holding the line, from there we held the line; we were subject to a couple of counter attacks which we soon disposed of.

- Brussels Sprout No.27 16th September- 17th September 1944: Back to rest area behind the canal at Lindel then at Neerpelt. **Brussels Sprout Diary**

On the 17th September the Operation Market Garden took place which was the airborne landing at Arnhem, Holland. Now then the Guards Armoured Division were detailed to break out over the canal and into Holland on the way up to Arnhem and the Irish Guards Tanks were gonna lead, we should have gone over and we were to bash through up to Nijmegan and then go onto Arnhem. The British Paratroopers had landed at Arnhem, and the American 101st Airborne landed in different places along the route, some landed to the right of Nijmegan, that was the 82nd Airborne it overlooked the Reichswalde Forest, they captured the Grave Bridge and various areas along the route, there was a different bridge, it was longer and the American Paratroopers had dropped on and captured these y'see. It was brilliantly done, they captured the bridge in tact and what not and of course our lads landed at the same time and the break out started. So we were to follow the Irish Guards over and we were to have close support by Spitfires and Typhoons who were to knock the opposition out that was in front of them and if there were any Tanks they were to go in and blast what they could and we could just bash on along what they called this 'Centre Route.'

- The Brussels Sprout No 30. 20th September 1944: In counter attack role with 82nd U.S Airborne Division. **Brussel Sprout Diary No 33.**

We carried on, we did very well the engineers had built bridges and so forth, we got up to the 82nd Airborne Division who were ready to do an attack over the river and outflank Nijmegan, but unfortunately for the Irish Guards across the canal on their way to Eindhoven there was an 88mm squat and the first six Mish Guard Tanks got knocked out all in a line y'see, so it was the following day that we crossed over and continued the march. Of course we'd been held up, so instead of following straight over we were now 24 hours late going over y'see, so that was the start of the rot as I saw it, it was the start of the rot for not getting to Arnhem, although saying that I didn't think they would have gotten through to Arnhem, we'd have probably got a day early to Nijmegan but getting to Arnhem from Nijmegan was almost impossible, well it was impossible with the tanks because there was one road and it was all built up and off the road the tanks just sank, there was no way they could operate y'see so they were held there and we were frustrated.

- Brussels Sprout No.32 25th September – 30th September 1944: Remainder of battalion astride Grave – Heesch Rd.
  Brussels Sprout Diary

Anyway we'd travelled along and we kept meeting the American Infantry and the American Airborne and we finished up on the edge of the Reichswalde Forest to the right of Nijmegan, we linked up with the American Airborne there and our tanks supported them as the Americans did an attack against the River Waal. Aye, as I say funny things happened, we'd linked up to the American Airborne, and we'd harboured for the night, so we'd pulled off the track into some woods, I heard this here firing at the back of us and I thought it must have been a German Tank, anyway it was a Messerschmitt and he were coming right down the column y'know like, well my mate he dived under a carrier and I cleared this 'ere thorn hedge, I felt something sharp stab me right in the backside and I thought,

'Oh I've got me blighty' I turned to me mate and said 'How bad is it, how bad is it?' he said

'Oh ya big soft buggar ere.' and he handed me a thorn, a

thorn about four or five inches long, it were stuck in me bum like, so that were my blighty. Aye me mate he dived under a carrier and they use to fire a mixture of high explosives, phosphors and what not, he'd lost some fingers y'know with the phosphors and so on, his clothes were burning, Dougie Adams they called him, of course he were home then and got his blighty.

Our tanks went into Nijmegan with a bit of fighting the Grenadier's Tanks they dashed over firing, there were chaps up on the rigging of the bridge all explosives ready and a Tank it crashed across the bridge shooting the fellas in the rafters and what not and we eventually captured the bridge. It was a massive, massive bridge it was the Nijmegan Bridge now called The Grenadiers Bridge because it was a Grenadier Tank that crashed over fighting y'see. They cleared the bridge and dismantled the explosives and we managed to get over as far as we could go to a little village called Elst. So after this fighting in Nijmegan and clearing the town we crossed over and we went sort of right off from the road which led to Arnhem and headed to Elst.

We were holding the ground round and about it like and the SS were still in the area so we were holding still, but we couldn't get through this main route to Arnhem and it finished up, I think it was the Second Regiment who went in late at night and got what was left of the Paras back out y'see. We knew things weren't going too well for the Para's, as a couple of days after the first landing the Polish Paratroopers came in and they were been fired at as they were Para-shooting in, the planes were been hit and you could see them going down, Dakotas like, like I say eventually when the perimeter closed up they did evacuate the very few that were left of the Paratroopers Division, the Regiment that had gone in at night time made an area for the ones that were able to come back from Arnhem to cross the river.

Now, then we moved about the different parts of the front,

there was one incident I remember, we were based in our Office, placed in our positions, it was night time, a freezing misty moonlit night in September, we were told

'There's nothing in front of you only Germans.'

So we saw just in front of our position there was a Gun Tractor what they called a Porte, my gunner Horace Camm, been a man of initiative looking for the opportunity of loot went scrounging round this vehicle, he came back with cushions out of it and tins of food and what not so we were doing very nicely, anyway we did our usual night time Guard and Sentry. At first light in the morning we did a stand to, everybody was up and awake at their gun positions, out of the mist came this here little Artillery Sergeant went to his truck and he absolutely exploded, our section sergeant who we called Jimmy Dimment, he'd no neck and he was built like a bull, he was known as Bull Dimment and he was a massive man, so this little Artillery Sergeant comes up and he had his Bren Gun, he was complaining bitterly about his stuff that had gone missing and he says to Bull Dimment,

'If that stuff isn't back in that truck in two minutes I'm going to ram this Bren Gun up your bloody arse.' Imagine the spectacle of a big gruff Guard Sergeant and a little Artillery Sergeant; it really was one amusing incident.

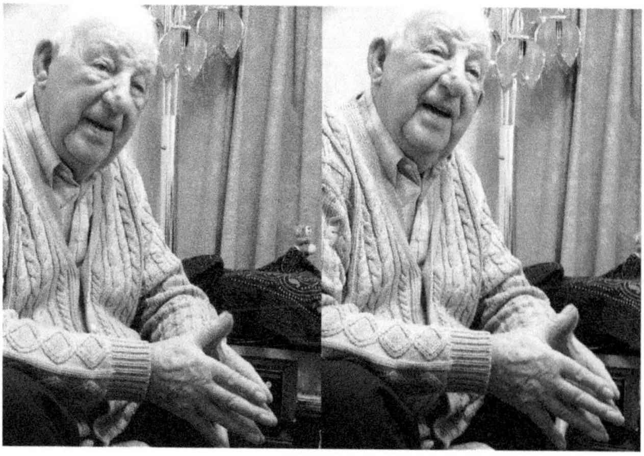

Over on our left flank the following day the Irish Guards had gone into action and taken a heavy beating, they met up with German Paratroopers some equipped with flame throwers and they suffered a lot of casualties so they were relieved that they were brought outta the line. The Commanding Officer led us himself that particular night, along this here track and the whole Carrier Platoon, we were taken through into a position and we were told to dig in, in this orchard or at the edge of it. We'd to dig gun positions and our carriers were held back in the orchard on this farmyard, we'd to dig a crawl trench, well all night long we dug and it was like concrete by the time we were done my hands were like concrete too y'know, in fact by the time we'd done my hands were bleeding, not only that, we had to put up with the German line only about 100 yards away across this field y'know. They were dug in and our artillery were dropping things in on them, it was the big guns that they were firing with what we call the five, which fired 100lb shells, when they were coming in they were just sounding like an express train coming over you y'know, they were bursting and we were all living in hope none would drop short and drop on us you see, there was somebody in the German line, his nerves must have gone we could hear him shouting all night long y'know.

After stand to we'd dug pits and we run the carriers over which was fortunate, we'd left lads on the gun positions and the remainder of us came back and prepared a breakfast like for all of us, cos under the carriers we had the cookers, they must have realised we were the cause of the Artillery barrage and they put down a fierce barrage on the orchard, but we were all safe cos we were under cover y'see like.

That was just the one time, we were there three days and three more troops had come up and we were brought out of the line to refit, we were living in the farmhouses and the barns and what not y'know. That was just outside Nijmegan we were there possibly a week refitting and we restocked and what not.

- The battalion then moved to, and dug into, the area known as 'The Island' between Nijmegan and Arnhem, more specifically an area known as 'Stonk Hill' due to the extremely heavy levels of German artillery targeting the position. From here the 5th battalion was key in holding the gains that had been made in the area from German counterattacks.
  History of the 5th Bn Coldstream Guards
  www.5thbncoldstreamguards.com

- Brussels Sprout No.35 7th October – 9th October 1944:
  To rest area west of Maas, Waal Canal.
  Brussels Sprout Diary

- Brussels Sprout No.36 10th October – 3rd November 1944:
  To rest area east of Maas, Waal Canal, Hatert.
  Brussels Sprout Diary

I know it sounds horrible, but you got so case hardened if you know what I mean, you felt it if one of your own lads were dying or had died and as I say you used to think,

'Well thank fuck it wasn't me, I'm glad it wasn't me' and you would do what you could for them.

You know we were in a barn and Rifle Company had gone forward, there were no use for the Carriers we were set up around this here farm and Tommy Witton was my section Sergeant at this particular time. The barn roof went that way and the farmhouse roof went that way, there was a big type of threshing machine, so we'd pushed that in the enemy side and we use to kip down the side here y'see and this bloody shell came over and ooh it must have just skimmed our barn like that and it landed on the apex of the roof of this farm. Now then dug in on't side were these 'ere support lads Northumberland Fusiliers, the machine gun section, the blast hit 3 or 4 of them and killed them, there were one of our lads killed, he was a young fella, I didn't get to know him, he was a sort of a loner, and it had killed him. Well I dashes into the farm house and one of our young officers had been upstairs and he'd got blasts all round well we got him out and there's this other lad and he said

'I got hit' and there was blood running down his sleeve, I said

'It's got him in the arm' So I put a dressing on and he was still bleeding so I says

'Get your blouse off' and he had a piece in his shoulder as well like y'see, shrapnel.

There was another lad killed in it but we couldn't do owt for him, so I took him over to, it was like a little chapel, church place where RAP was so I got this here lad over to it and got him in and on a table, this lad he hadn't a stitch on him and he was absolutely covered in holes, blood oozing out of them and he was just left there, there were that many wounds they couldn't do owt for him he just bled to death did the poor lad, he must have got the full blast of it y'know it covered his body from his legs up to his face. You just get on with it though that's all you can do and as I say, I'm speaking for myself but you got case hardened and use to think to myself,

'Thank fuck it wasn't me.' I suppose it was a selfish attitude, self preservation.

Another incident I got caught out, we were in our gun positions in an orchard overlooking a valley and Captain Fanning had his little HQ across the road in the corner of a field, he said,

'Come with me Sergeant, I'll show you where I'm dug in if you need to get in touch with me you know where I am.'

So he climbed over the gate and just at that instance I heard the howling, the winding up and as I say once you'd experienced them you'd a fair idea where the buggars were coming and I could hear them zinging and I dived down the back of this hedge and of course old Percy got away. First one landed it was right on the bloody line with this hedge and I thought,

'Oh Christ if it comes this way I've had it.' But no, they went t'other way in a line, well my arsehole it were like that y'know, and I was over that bloody fence.

'Are you alright?' said Captain Fanning.

'Yes Sir.'

The following morning we were dug on forward, we'd parked the carriers at the rear and the drill was at Stand To everybody was up and alert, so I tried to be alert and you were in your gun position, that was just as daylight was just twitching in the sky. Until it were clear and then you could stand down, you'd leave the lads on gun positions go back to where the Carriers were and you'd get the grub on and relieve them and let them have a meal. So it was a beautiful morning and the mail had come the night before and Beryl's Dad used to send me the Evening Post. So I'm sat at the side of the Carrier I gets paper out, oh it were lovely, beautiful morning, I'd had a right nice breakfast y'know and I heard crack, crack, crack, crack, I thought 'the buggars coming this way' and they did. One landed at the top end of the orchard and they were bursting in the apple trees like y'see, I tried to get under the Carrier but it was that weighted down with gear I couldn't and I were like huddled down here and as soon as they'd landed I was off I'd have given Jessie Owens at 100 yards and I'd have beat him up this track, my bloody heart were pounding and pumping and I dived into my trench. There were a lad called Harvey in the next trench and he come over and he said,

'Ere have a look at me.' And a bit of Shrapnel had just sliced his ribs like and he'd been in his trench, so I bandaged him up like and I said,

'Are you going to the MO.'

'No I shall be alright, I'll keep an eye on it.'

It had just sliced him like and he soldiered on did the lad, even then you could laugh about it, poor old Horace, we were all smitten with diarrhoea and runs, Carrier stopped Horace grabbed shovel and his away over, and he comes slithering back,

'Oh I'm too late' he said and he'd shit himself like y'know.

And we used to kid him on,

'Who'd shit himself or who'd been fired at?' Like y'know, they use to do a bit of leg pulling y'know it was alright. Well I suppose the Germans had their characters too, I tell you what when you were over a runner position it were a dash to get into their bunkers mind, you could tell where they'd been there was a horrible sickly, scenty smell where they'd been enclosed and there were these French pictures all the way round the bunkers y'know of nude ladies and what not, they were buggars for them were the Germans like, we were trying to get first in to grab them.

'Grandad burst into laughter so much he had a coughing fit'

Then on the 4th November we went into the line and we took over from a Rifle Brigade Battalion in Overloon we were ordered to move out and take over their positions, we had to take over in daylight and we were observed all the time apparently, Captain Fanning our Platoon Officer he was killed that day. He was out reccy'ing (reconnaissance) and he was trench mortared, he was killed was Captain Fanning. My pal Billy Wigglesworth he got a wound in his bum, he got a 'Blighty' and was sent back to England.

- After its beating at 'Stonk Hill', the battalion was rewarded with 3 weeks in Hatert. However after this, the battalion was flung straight back into thick fighting, relieving elements of the 11th armoured division in fighting around the Maas pocket against the German 7th and 102nd Fallschirmjager (paratrooper) Regiments.
  History of the 5th Bn Coldstream Guards
  www.5thbncoldstreamguards.com

- Brussels Sprout No.37 4th November – 11th November 1944: Battalion to defensive position in MAAS pocket, area Leune. Here relieved Motor Battalion of 11th Armoured for rest. **Brussels Sprout Diary**

'Grandad let out a big horrible groan at the next memory.'

On November 4th we took over and facing us was the SS again and the Dutch SS y'know and we used to get shelled with machine guns on a night time and oh it was one of the most depressing places y'know. It rained and rained it was soggy and right depressing countryside like, it truly was one of the most depressing places I'd been and I was really under the weather, well we all were like, it was a most depressing place a lot of the first night we were dug in and it was miserable rainy and a right dismal out look. During the night a German patrol had come in and they snatched a lad outta the trench who unfortunately had a map on him marking the minefield and the path through it. So the next night a German Fighting

Patrol came through about thirty strong, went right through to our soft vehicles which were way back with our petrol and so on and they had created a bit of mayhem y'know.

Well we found out that they got through the back through the minefield, so what happened was we'd thirteen Bren guns in our platoon, six two inch mortars and we were dug in at this side and then the companies were dug in on the other side, then what we did was we made a perimeter with all the mortars with flares and waited. The Patrol went out and they were lying in wait and when they saw activity starting with the Germans they came back and bolted, so they got into the middle of the mine field and they sent flares up well all these mortars opened up with flares, and we caught the Germans right in the mine fields, and all the Bren guns gave 'em some stick like, well that frightened them, they never came anymore, they never came back that way, we inflicted a lot of casualties on them y'see.

While we were there, it was obviously deserted and every morning our Artillery Spotters would go up into the steeple, each morning there was an SP Gun (self-propelled) would open out and bang a couple of shells at the church like. So anyway we were in position and we could smell this here lovely smell of cooking pork, we went to see where this lovely smell was coming from and old Horace as usual been on the trail had been out rooting and it was a lad called Paddy Cox in another section he'd killed a little pig an butchered it and were roasting it like y'see, so of course we got the idea. There were lots of little pigs running about and they'd have been killed or they'd have died of starvation, so it was a treat for us and a blessing for them that we'd killed these little pigs. We all got quite adept at been butchers so we could kill a pig and have it butchered in quick time. Horace had been doing his usual round and he'd been in to see a, well I don't know if it had been a shop or something, anyways he came in with these little cartons and we didn't know what they were, they looked like oats so we said it were like Quaker oats y'see. So the next morning we had the Big Dixie on the boil and we started pouring these flakes in, anyway it turned out it were a lovely porridge, so he'd discovered some honey had Horace and we had food containers which we filled with honey, we use to pour the honey in with the oats and coming out of the trenches after all night y'know it was a real treat. So what with Horace's Quaker oats, and Paddy Cox's little pigs we lived very well.

Brussels liberation flowers.

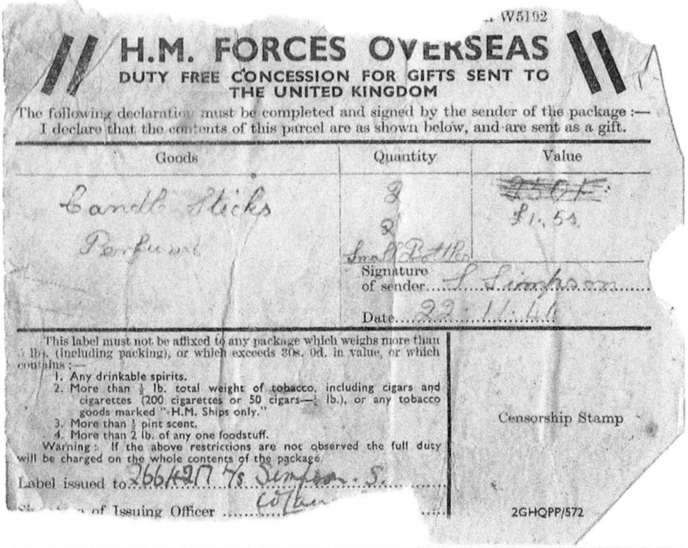

W5192

H.M. FORCES OVERSEAS

DUTY FREE CONCESSION FOR GIFTS SENT TO THE UNITED KINGDOM

The following declaration must be completed and signed by the sender of the package :—
I declare that the contents of this parcel are as shown below, and are sent as a gift.

Goods	Quantity	Value
Candle Sticks	2	~~250 F~~ £1. 5.
Perfume	2 Small Bottles	

Signature of sender....S. Simpson....

Date....22 . 11 . 44....

This label must not be affixed to any package which weighs more than .. lbs. (including packing), or which exceeds 30s. 0d. in value, or which contains :—

1. Any drinkable spirits.
2. More than ½ lb. total weight of tobacco, including cigars and cigarettes (200 cigarettes or 50 cigars—½ lb.), or any tobacco goods marked "H.M. Ships only."
3. More than ½ pint scent.
4. More than 2 lb. of any one foodstuff.

Warning : If the above restrictions are not observed the full duty will be charged on the whole contents of the package.

Label issued to....2661217 Pte Simpson. S....

... of Issuing Officer ....

Censorship Stamp

2GHQPP/572

(Army Form A. 2042.
R.A.F. Form No. 1929)

FIELD SERVICE

POST CARD

POST OFFICE 10 NO 44

The address only to be written on this side. If anything else is added the post card will be destroyed.

(Crown Copyright Reserved.)

To Miss D. Clough
122 Hetton Road,
off Easterly Road,
Harehills,
Leeds 8, Yorks,
England.

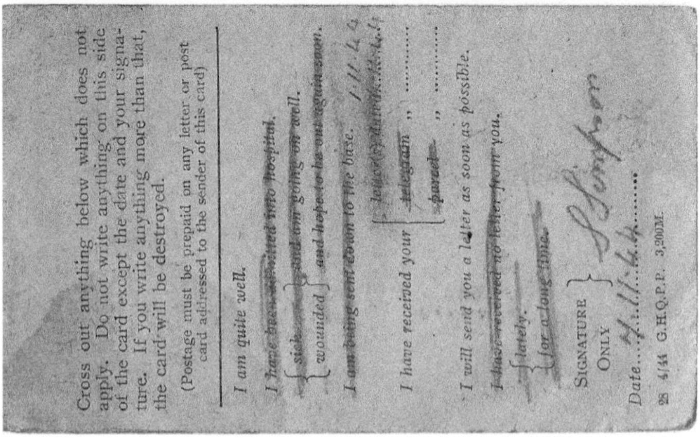

Cross out anything below which does not apply. Do not write anything on this side of the card except the date and your signature. If you write anything more than that, the card will be destroyed.

(Postage must be prepaid on any letter or post card addressed to the sender of this card)

I am quite well.

~~*I have been admitted into hospital.*~~

~~*sick*~~ } ~~*and am going on well.*~~
~~*wounded*~~ } ~~*and hope to be out again soon.*~~

~~*I am being sent down to the base.*~~ 1/11/44

I have received your { ~~*letter dated*~~ .... ~~*telegram*~~ ,, ... ~~*parcel*~~ ,, ... }

I will send you a letter as soon as possible.

~~*I have received no letter from you*~~ { ~~*lately.*~~ ~~*for a long time.*~~ }

SIGNATURE ONLY } S Simpson

Date....1/11/44....

28 4/44 G.H.Q.P.P. 3,200M.

A Christmas card sent to Beryl from Steve reading; 'From Steve with love and best wishes. Xxx'

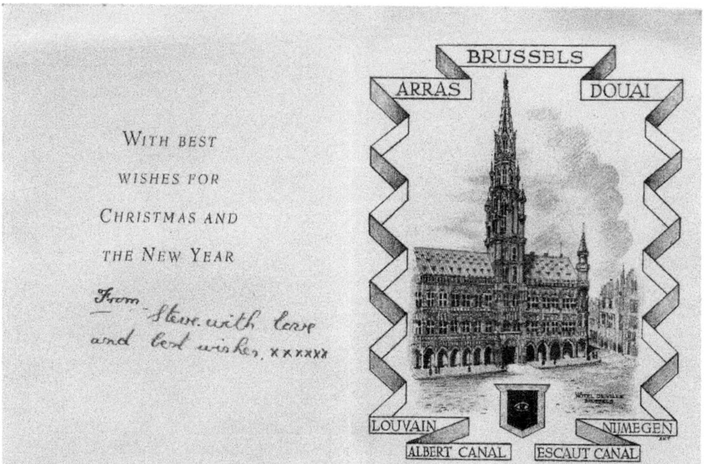

Top facing page: this postal docket lists 2 x Candle Sticks and 2 x Perfume were posted on 22nd November 1944. The bottles of perfume had survived the recent hard fighting somehow and Steve posted them on as promised back in the September to Beryl.

Bottom facing page: both sides of a field postcard posted to Beryl 7th November 1944 highlighted 'I am quite well. I will send you a letter as soon as possible.'

6

'A GERMAN SECRET WEAPON OLD LAD!'

So from there we came out at Nijmegan after a very nervous period in that line, we moved on and we moved to a different part of the front, for a few days then we went down further into Holland to a place called Sittard and we crossed the German border at a place called Verviers it was the end of where the American Line was and we took over from the American Scout Guard Regiment and of course they pulled back and returned to their own area.

- Brussels Sprout No.38 11th November – 20th December 1944: Guards Armoured Division take over Sittard sector from U.S Battalion in area of Weir..
  Brussels Sprout Diary

It was over the Dutch, German border it was a massive area, a massive pine forest, a terrific pine forest and we were dug in at the end, there was a valley and a sort of a township in the distance and one of our young Patrol Officers took a patrol out the first night, unfortunately he went onto a minefield and we could hear him screaming and crying all night long, he died, we had to leave him and we couldn't go get him, that was hard.

It was Gelsenkirchen was the town that we could see further over, well of course we were gonna attack it and take over but things changed and we were there for about two or three weeks, while we were there we put a lot of trick players out and what not, booby-traps, the Americans had done a lot as well and you'd to be very careful because we didn't know where theirs were for sure like. There was a lot of German Patrol Activity and sometimes they'd have a dog and they'd send a dog out, we realised what was going off and we'd stay right quiet and still and we didn't do anything, the dog would go off again like. We sent a lot of patrols out, it was a bit hairy and you had to be very careful, in fact no body dare get outta the trenches on a night because if there was any movement somebody would open up and fire at them like y'know, you didn't know whether it was Germans so we always stayed in the trenches and said if there was anybody moving it was enemy so you could open up and fire legitimately.

There was an amusing incident I'll tell you about with Horace, we used to share the same trench like, well we use to take it in turns where you'd do two hours off and then it would be your turn to do two-hour sentry on y'see and then the next trench would do two hours and so on. Well this particular night Horace and I are sharing the same trench and he complained that he wanted to go to the loo sort of thing; he said he wanted a clear out, I said,

'Nip over the back Horace' he said,

'No I might get a bullet in my arse!' So he's moaning away there then he says 'I gotta go Sarg.' I goes,

'Well get your shovel and do it on't shovel' while he's in't trench y'see, so he had a right good clear out did Horace like and he did himself up and he says,

'What shall I do with it?'

'Well I don't want it for a pack up Horace, so sling it' thinking he'd throw it over the back and then he could bury it the next morning, but no, he slung it and it dropped to the side, he'd slung it and it dropped into the next trench. So there was peace for a minute and then there was such a screech and a shout and it was blood and thunder from't next trench, a lad called Shuttleworth it had dropped on. Next morning after stand to we'd go back to do cooking or what not and Shuttleworth there come out smelling of roses, he wanted to know what had gone on so I told him,

'It must have been a German secret weapon old lad and I'm glad to say it wasn't me' anyway it died a peaceful death. Aye Horace Camm he was a Doncaster boy, I asked if anyone knew him but nobody did.

After holding the line at Verviers for a couple of weeks we were due to be relieved by an Infantry Regiment as we had to make for Louvain near Brussels for the armour to be refitted. Unfortunately the Germans started the high density Ardennes Offensive so we were hurriedly sent down to that part of the front, our objective was a place called Namur which was in the line of the German advance. Now then we were supposed to be holding the position there and meet the Germans if they came through, the weather was atrocious, frost and fog really savage frost it was, suddenly the weather cleared and the bombers went in and really pasted the Germans.

- Brussels Sprout No.39 21st December 1944:
  German Ardennes offensive. Move to Opheylissem.
  Brussels Sprout Diary

Christmas Eve then and we were at a place called Neerheylissem near Belgium, we were going to stay with civilians in their homes who were going to accommodate us, we got into theses villages, our battalions and tank battalions an so on into Opheylissem and Neerheylissem. Well I was billeted with my friend Tommy Musgrove in this house and there was this Grandmother, her daughter with her little girl Janine and her husband Louis. Well we were only there two nights and we were called out Christmas Eve we'd an hours notice to move down to Namur and the Germans were pushing through. Christmas Eve we got the warning to stand by to move, well we were waiting all night long and like I said the frost was savage really savage. On Christmas morning itself we were ordered to move down to Namur, the Germans were trying to get through the middle to cut us in two and get to Antwerp you see.

- Brussels Sprout No.40 25th December – 27th December 1944: Took over protection of bridge at Namur.
  Brussels Sprout Diary

If they'd had got through there they'd have caused a lot of bloody problems so as I say the Americans were slogging it out at Bastogne and we'd to move in as a block y'see. We were holding the line Christmas day on Christmas morning we'd moved down and it was freezing, bone chilling frozen, you'd sit in the Carrier and I'm not kidding you'd sit in the Carrier with your head just peeping out and the frost on your eyebrows it was that thick y'know, it was absolutely bone chilling freezing cold. Anyway Christmas night we got bombed and they blew the railway bridge, the skies cleared on that particular morning and the bombers came in and of course they knocked the shit outta the Germans then like, of course it stopped the break out and eventually they were forced back. As I say the bombers went in and smacked the Germans so that was possibly the end of the breakout and them trying to cut into the army and get to Antwerp. Old Monty took charge of the area and he got it all sorted did old Monty, (General Montgomery), he took over from me that part of the sector, got things organised did t'old lad.

So we went back to our billets then like in this place called Neerheylissem in Belgium and we were there about a month with these people, the civilians offered us accommodation, somewhere to sleep y'see in a house, they were very nice you know and it was just like leaving home when we had to leave.

- Brussels Sprout No.41 27th December 1944 – 7th February 1945: Back to Opheylissem for long rest.
  Brussels Sprout Diary

For a month we did training and got the vehicles ready again then at end of January the big attack started into the Reichswalde Forest, intending to cross into Germany we were ordered to move, all the population turned out of Neerheylissem, it was like leaving home, they were lovely people. I have fond memories of them; in fact I called my eldest daughter Jannine, after the little girl where I was billeted.

'At this point in the interview Grandad broke down and cried, through his tears he told me about how he had named his own daughter after the little girl he was billeted with. In 1984 he surprised the same family and revisited his old billet.'

- Brussels Sprout No.42 – No.43 7th February – 12th February 1945: To Harlen, concentration area for operation 'Veritable'. Closing up to Nijmegan.
  Brussels Sprout Diary

- The beginning of 1945 saw the 5th moving back to the Nijmegan area for operation 'Veritable'. Elements of the division, including the 5th, launched attacks on Mull with fierce fighting punctuated by heavy artillery barrages known as 'Stonks', on the advancing guards. After victory here, the 5th was rested in Schule from the 23rd of February to the 3rd of March.
  History of the 5th Bn Coldstream Guards
  www.5thbncoldstreamguards.com

We left in February and that's when the big offensive started from Nijmegan, we moved out and it was very difficult as it was all waterlogged with the rain, but eventually the infantry lads broke through to the Nijmegan area through the Reichswalde Forest to Germany itself. We were fighting on German soil then so it didn't matter about battering the buildings and all that, we fought through Goch and Kleve and into Germany. The armour was able to carry on and then we battled on till eventually we did a final action to a place called Wesel on the Rhine. That was the end of the battles in our part of the country, it was an awful battle, a lot of casualties, there was a lot of bravery; some of 'em wouldn't go where the infantry had to go.

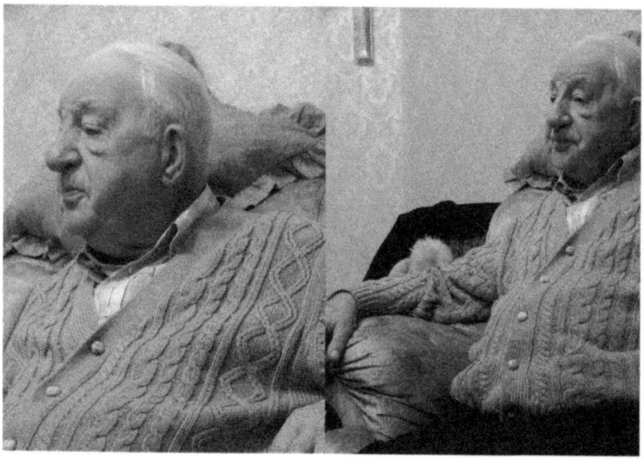

'Here Grandad's voice started to break again, he took another long pause to collect himself, he wanted to finish the story, it had to be told, as painful as the memories were for him'.

- Brussels Sprout No.44 – No.46 13th February – 21st February 1945:
  Closing up to battle, move to Groesbeek. Under command 51 Division attack to enlarge Gennep bridge head over Niers. Second attack captured Mull.
  Brussels Sprout Diary

That was a real test, tanks and all sorts had tried it, they shoved our 5th Battalion in and eventually, we had a hell of a lot of casualties, but eventually we cleared it and that was the Rhine cleared up y'see, anyway we finally cracked it and that was the end of the campaign so far, at a place called Wesel. From there we were pulled back to a harbour area, refitted and re-kitted again.

Then in April for the build up there was a terrific smoke screen right along our section of the front, so for about two weeks they'd massive smoke screens right along the front like, a big smoke screen as they were building up at the back with the bridging equipment and all sorts of assault equipment y'know. It was all been built up and then they did an assault crossing across the river which was 1000 yards wide at the time, they built a bridge across it 1000 yards long was the bridge the engineers had built. The Paratroopers had landed the other side, there had been some right battling.

Anyway we crossed over and we swung on into Germany till eventually we got up to round about the Rotenberg area when the war finished, anyway it was different little places with a lot of fighting, a lot of movement.

- Brussels Sprout No.47 22nd February 1945:
  Rest at Hommersum.
  Brussels Sprout Diary

- Brussels Sprout No. 50. 9th March 1945:
  Attacked through 2nd Scots Guards to Wesel. Bridgehead.
  Brussels Sprout Diary

- The next operation involved most of the division capturing the high ground at Bonninghardt; facing them was the 8th German Fallschirmjager Regiment.
  The 9th of March saw the 5th preparing to clear the Rhine bridge-head against fanatical resistance from the German 7th Fallschirmjager. Heavy fighting ensued, with the 5th taking heavy casualties before being pulled back to Mook for rest.

On the 24th of March the battalion once again paired up with the 1st Battalion Coldstream and began the push into Germany, meeting consistent and steady opposition. Reaching Enschek, where the battalion's Victoria Cross of the war was won by Lieutenant Ian Liddell.

From here the battalion moved through Remsel, Thuine to Berge and on the 11th of April helped force a crossing over the river Haze with heavy fighting at Bohah and Bren. On the 22nd of April, the 5th moved into Rothenburg and then through to Zeven where short lived but fierce fighting erupted against the 15th Panzer Division

History of the 5th Bn Coldstream Guards www.5thbncoldstreamguards.com

'In his collection Grandad kept a newspaper cutting from The Times 23rd March 1945.'

THE TIMES FRIDAY 23RD MARCH 1945
THE GUARDS IN ACTION

'The last act in the clearance of the German Bridgehead west of the Rhine at Wesel was marked by a heroic episode which fitly closed one of the hardest fought soldiers' battles of this war. As an example of disciplined valour, of that "majesty" which NAPIER attributes to the British soldier, it could not have been surpassed. War may have become a thing of machinery, of armour, of fire power, but occasions will always arise which call for the supreme daring of the infantry assault, and no belligerent nation which cannot breed and train men capable o facing that test can hope to clinch its victories, however formidable the material by which they are prepared. The Coldstream Guards advanced under a hail of fire from front and flanks, some of it directed from houses not 100 yards distant. For 1,500 yards they fought their way forward against furious resistance.

"I closed my turret, a thing I have never done before" said a tank Sergeant who was watching. "I myself was inside four inches of steel and still wasn't too happy, yet those boys did not seem to know what fear was." The guardsmen dashed across bullet swept open ground. They cleared buildings storey by storey and room by room. Their opponents consisted of the fiercest troops in the German Army, but in the end their resistance broke and they gave way, while the Coldstreamers avenged their losses by pouring a stream of fire into retreating ranks.

There exist great traditions in the British Army and many magnificent individual regimental traditions, which create at once a responsibility and an inspiration. Perhaps the essential tradition of the Brigade if Guards has been the almost uncanny steadiness and imperturbability which has made it the *triarii* of the Army, the final resort of the British Commander against the hard core of resistance which it seems almost impossible to break, or to restore the fortunes of a day that threatens to turn out ill, or in the deepest adversity of defeat and retreat avert disaster. To these tasks guardsmen are reared; to these spurs they never fail to respond. And their store of abnegation is never plumbed byt eh hardest task. Yet it is abnegation, not fanaticism.

In this last assault of the Wesel Bridgehead the Coldstream Guards encountered true fanatics, the parachute battalions indoctrinated with all the racial myths and pagan ideologies designed to turn men into killing machines and all too successful in their application. That is one way to form Hrd fighting

Above: Smoke screen

soldier. The men who met and beat the Parachutists were formed and nurtured on drill and discipline, minor tactics, and the honour and duty of guardsman. They have carried their courage and efficiency into many campaigns of the war, but they have borne along with it their good behaviour and friendliness. Their pride is a wholesome tonic, devoid of arrogance. They have not been dehumanized by the hard school through which they have passed or made unsuited for citizenship. The final action in the Wesel bridgehead proves once more that if the men of free peoples will endure the hardening which war demands they can outmatch the chosen product of a killer caste.'
Printed by The Times Publishing Company, Ltd, England.

- Brussels Sprout No.68 22nd April 1945:
Joint Coldstream/Scots Guards attack captures Rottenburg.
Brussels Sprout Diary

Left:
Nijmegan
bridge

Right:
Wesel
Bridge

Leading Article Reprinted from

THE TIMES

Friday March 23 1945

The Guards in Action

The last act in the clearance of the German bridgehead west of the Rhine at Wesel was marked by a heroic episode which fitly closed one of the hardest-fought soldiers' battles of this war. As an example of disciplined valour, of that "majesty" which NAPIER attributes to the British soldier, it could not have been surpassed. War may become a thing of machinery, of armour, of fire-power, but occasions will always arise which call for the supreme daring of the infantry assault, and no belligerent nation which cannot breed and train men capable of facing that test can hope to clinch its victories, however formidable the material by which they are prepared. The Coldstream Guards advanced under a hail of fire from front and flanks, some of it directed from houses not 100 yards distant. For 1,500 yards they fought their way forward against furious resistance. "I closed down my turret, "a thing I have never done before," said a tank sergeant who was watching. "I myself was inside four inches of steel "and still wasn't too happy, yet those boys "did not seem to know what fear was." The guardsmen dashed across bullet-swept open ground. They cleared buildings storey by storey and room by room. Their opponents consisted of the fiercest troops in the German Army, but in the end their resistance broke and they gave way, while the Coldstreamers avenged their losses by pouring a stream of fire into the retreating ranks.

There exist great traditions in the British Army and many magnificent individual regimental traditions, which create at once a responsibility and an inspiration. Perhaps the essential tradition of the Brigade of Guards has been the almost uncanny steadiness and imperturbability which has made it the *triarii* of the Army, the final resort of the British commander against the hard core of resistance which it seems almost impossible to break, or to restore the fortunes of a day that threatens to turn out ill, or in the deepest adversity of defeat and retreat to avert disaster. To these tasks guardsmen are reared; to these spurs they never fail to respond. And their store of abnegation is never plumbed by the hardest task. Yet it is abnegation, not fanaticism. In this last assault on the Wesel bridgehead the Coldstream Guards encountered true fanatics, the Parachute battalions indoctrinated with all the racial myths and pagan ideologies designed to turn men into killing machines and all too successful in their application. That is one way to form a hard-fighting soldier. The men who met and beat the Parachutists were formed and nurtured on drill and discipline, minor tactics, and the honour and duty of a guardsman. They have carried their courage and efficiency into many campaigns of the war, but they have borne along with it their good behaviour and friendliness. Their pride is a wholesome tonic, devoid of arrogance. They have not been dehumanized by the hard school through which they have passed or made unsuited for citizenship. The final action in the Wesel bridgehead proves once more that if the men of free peoples will endure the hardening which war demands they can outmatch the chosen product of a killer caste.

Printed by THE TIMES PUBLISHING COMPANY, Limited, Printing House Square, London, E.C.4, England.

The newspaper clipping describing in more detail the battle around Wesel it is dated March 23rd 1945.

Above: Wesel

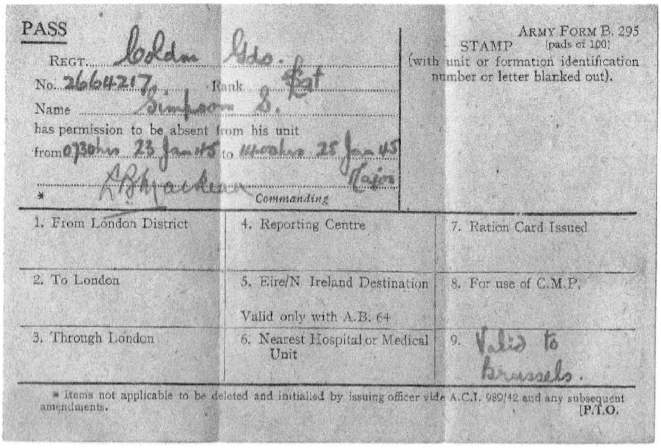

PASS

ARMY FORM B. 295

REGT. Coldm Gds.

No. 2664217 Rank

Name Simpson S.

has permission to be absent from his unit

from 0730hrs 23 Jan 45 to 1400hrs 25 Jan 45

* Major Commanding

STAMP (pads of 100)
(with unit or formation identification number or letter blanked out).

1. From London District	4. Reporting Centre	7. Ration Card Issued
2. To London	5. Eire/N. Ireland Destination Valid only with A.B. 64	8. For use of C.M.P.
3. Through London	6. Nearest Hospital or Medical Unit	9. Valid to Brussels.

* Items not applicable to be deleted and initialled by issuing officer vide A.C.I. 989/42 and any subsequent amendments. [P.T.O.

Above: A pass for 2.5 days only 23rd January 1945 from 0730 hrs to 14oo hrs 25th January 1945 Valid to Brussels.

Below: Left – John England, right – Steve in Wesel with a Carrier.

Above: Madame Millie. This photograph was amongst Steve's large collection and is the lady who he was billeted with in 1944.

Three postcards of Nijmegan, found amongst Steve's collection. These were hard battles around this area yet here he is collecting souvenirs marking a nicer side of his journey, if there was one, he found it.

Original 1938 Nederlanden 1 Gulden bank note

7

'WE COULDN'T DO ANYTHING FOR THEM!'

It came to the end of April and leave had started, we had got well into the journey and my turn came for 7 days leave, so I came back to England, that was the first seven days leave I'd had in about 12 months.England looked very, very shabby did the country y'know, people were very weary they had had six years of war and rationing y'know like. I was, well people were pleased that it was over, it hadn't been easy for the civilians, you know there had been lots of hard times, they had had severe rationing and the people got through it and they had managed like. Their reaction to me was of no great joy, but they were pleased you'd got home safe like and everything was ok, some were sad that they had lost those they knew, but I don't think they begrudged it to you because you'd got through it alright y'know.

Anyway during that leave I got engaged to my wife, Beryl Clough, your Nana. I'd just said goodbye to Beryl after getting engaged, I tell you this I got down to Kingscross that's where I left Beryl and there was a notice up there and if you came on leave like from BLA you were given a draft number sort of thing and I saw my draft number and it said Leave Extended 2 Days. So I thought what am I gonna do? I know Pirbright, me old mate Billy Wigs down there (Wigglesworth) so I tootles off to Pirbright.

I goes up and across the road was a motorcycle shed opposite the Sergeants Mess and heard a,

'Eh up Marra how's it going, how ya doin?' and it were old Ned he'd been wounded early on so he were in stores at the motorcycle shed.

'Am alright old mate.' I says. I was Lance Sergeant then like I'd got promoted August 1944.

Well then I met Billy I went in and saw our RSM and he invited me in and I had a meal there like and I spent a night in London and then I was off on my draft then like. I wasn't looking forward to going back to any further campaigning, but in my mind I was saying,

'What's going to happen now? Because they were saying the war was almost over, the Americans had lanced up with the Russians. So it can't be that long now before its finished altogether.'

So I wasn't unduly worried about going back into it but my thought was how I've just left Beryl like.

We stayed a night at a transit camp in Calais and we got transport, when I returned to Germany it was just prior to the war finishing I joined the Battalion at a place called Osnabruck, then the lines had stopped and there was a German cavalry barracks that they were in. On that particular day Mr Churchill announced that the war with Germany had finished. Now then while I'd been away the lads had done a lot of advancing and taken a lot of casualties, it was a very subdued end of the war as far as we were concerned, there was no great jollification or anything y'know.

They had Churchill on speaking and he was saying as of the 8th May war hostilities were finished with the Germans, and do you know I didn't even have a glass of beer, it were absolutely flat there, there was no celebration or nothing, it were just like a Sunday, but the next morning I joined my battalion and we came to life a bit then like y'see.

From there they said we'd to stay in the positions where we were while they negotiated the German Army's surrendering. The line was held for 2 or 3 days till orders were issued to the Germans and then our Division were ordered to disarm a German Parachute Division.

- Brussels Sprout No.76 7th May 1945:
  Move to airfield south of Cuxhaven to incarcerate 7 Parachute Division.
  Brussels Sprout Diary

We'd to go to an aerodrome near Cuxhaven Northern Germany, so we got orders then to move to Cuxhaven where we were gonna disarm this Parachute Division and as I say it was a division we'd fought a few times like in our travels, they were ordered to stay where they were, with their arms and we were given a route to take to Cuxhaven Aerodrome and it was a route through them like.

Now then it was weird going through the German lines, the Germans were stood at their posts, we went through different places where they were still dug in and what not y'know like, in fact there was an armoured train and they were all stood there with the guns, it was weird driving through and seeing this great armoured train and Germans stood in gun positions and were thinking,

'It's a bit dodgy is this' y'know!'

We went through them onto the aerodrome and then the Germans had the order to march in and disarm on the airport, all the Arms were handed in; horses and carts etc and then the Officers were to be separated from the men. To say they were a defeated army you wouldn't have thought so; the column come marching in, and I saw a tall German Officer, Jack Booted! A typical German strutting there in front of his men and they're all marching away, well they come marching in he must have been 7ft this German Officer at the front he was a big man in his jack boots, he was there with his bloody Cain like a guards man, strutting along, he wasn't beaten. They were all marching in step at back of him was his troops and then heavy guns starting rolling in and track vehicles and what not and all the arms were piled up and then they sorted them out. These weren't SS these were ordinary Wehrmacht Soldiers like, the lads that would fight fair if they could if you know what I mean. They took the Officers to one side and ordinary soldiers to the other, well I suppose they were then taken to be interrogated and then depending on what information they had would have been sent on their way like or dealt with accordingly like, as for the soldiers,

'Are you a farmer?' they asked

'Yes'

'Piss off then, get off home.'

And that's how they dispersed them like, they'd to make their own way home like whether they lived at t'other side of Germany they were on their own to make it like. The Germans were just left to go I mean they were ordinary soldiers told what to do like, they weren't the villains, the SS or 'owt like that, the Gestapo and so forth were the villains; these were just ordinary fighting soldiers like we were.

The only one I truly came into contact with an SS man, you might think I'm exaggerating here now but I'm not it's as true as I'm sitting here, our intelligence sergeant they called him George Todd and the interpreter with him was a Dutch fella called Joff, he was a sergeant as well and he was from the Dutch army and I think he must have experienced some terrible things happening in his life to his family and he absolutely hated the Germans, you could feel it coming out of him y'know. So George is intelligence parked at other side of road and me and Tommy Witton with our section were at this side of the road, so we all let this bloke in.

'What you got?'

'Oh' he says 'He wants to die for thee Fuhrer.' and he was

one of these young SS and he looked a thug an all like. 'He's a good chance of dying for his Fuhrer.'

So anyway we goes back to the Carrier and we heard some shots, well we dashes over and he was in the ditch and Joff had put one through his head and we said,

'What's happened?'

'Oh he kicked me he tried to escape.'

Anyway you know they talk about premonitions, we were detailed, we were going to do a river crossing but fortunately one of our reccies found a bridge that was undamaged that we could get over so I'd been talking to George Todd and I just said

'Eh up mate how ya doing?' he says

'Do you know Steve I've got that feeling.'

'Oh don't talk bollocks George'

'No I've just got a feeling.'

And he went off in his truck and we heard an explosion and it was George he'd run over a bloody mine, blown up and killed him aye. We heard the mine go off, we heard the explosion and news came back George Todd has gone off over a mine he'd pulled off the curb, off the road y'know like.

- German forces surrendered in Europe and the 5th Battalion Coldstream Guards moved to Cuxhaven aerodrome to take the surrender of the 7th German Fallschirmjager Regiment, a unit the 5th had often fought against during its time in Europe.
  History of the 5th Bn Coldstream Guards www.5thbncoldstreamguards.com

- Brussels Sprout No.77 8th May 1945: V.E Day.
  Brussels Sprout Diary

Before we'd moved as an Armoured Division we were

disbanded, that was a sad day, it changed things y'see like anything that was disbanded it was like the end of an era sort of thing y'see, the 'Tankies' they were good lads they were our 1st Battalion, well there was the Irish Guards Tank Battalion, Grenadiers and Coldstream and they formed the Armoured Brigade y'see. Then there was our brigade of Irish Guards, Welsh Guards and us that was 32nd Guard Brigade and then there was the Brigade with the Artillery and all that sort of thing y'see. So when we were going into action and going to attack, you would form a battle group, the 5th Coldstream Tanks would be with the 1st Coldstream Tanks and you worked as a unit together like y'see. We did have some very brave fellas we had one VC, he stormed a bridge on his own which was manned with about 30 or 40 Germans, he stormed this bridge and there were machine guns firing at him he stormed this bridge on his own and he climbed the 6ft barrier, disarmed the bombs and what not and he got the VC. Captain Liddell they called him Ian Liddell.

- Lieutenant Ian Liddell single handily disarmed several large German aircraft bombs placed on the bridge by the Germans to destroy it, ensuring that British forces could continue their advances without delay. All of this was done by Lt. Liddell whilst under heavy small arms fire from German positions across the river; the Lieutenant had little cover and no support from his fellow guardsmen, also risking being blown to pieces by the bombs he was disarming. Miraculously he was uninjured.
  History of the 5th Bn Coldstream Guards www.5thbncoldstreamguards.com

Now then a fortnight after and a bloody sniper shot him and killed him aye, but that was bravery was that, Captain Liddell. So in the June it was decided the 5th Battalion would be disbanded like I say, well I took part in the parade, which was very sad. A photograph was taken of the Battalion, or should I say the remainder of the old 5th Battalion when it was formed, as I say I think there were about 120 of us, the remainder were reinforcements like. It was sad was because for four years a lot of us had soldiered together, you could say you loved some better than your own family, well some were family like, y'know. Great lads they were, anyway come the dispersal of the old 5th Battalion, we took part with lots of sports.

'At the memory of the Farewell To Armour Parade Grandad got upset again, he welled with mixed emotions.'

- At the start of the war the battalion was made up of 850 officers, non commissioned officers and other ranks; during its fighting career in Europe, from the 26th of June 1944 till VE day May 1945 a time of just under 9 months, it suffered 228 battlefield killed, 27% of the original battalion's strength. This figure excludes those who were left with injuries which left them unable to continue fighting.
  History of the 5th Bn Coldstream Guards www.5thbncoldstreamguards.com

- **The Guards Armoured Division. Farewell To Armour Parade. Rotenburg Airfield, Germany 9th June 1945.**
  Field Marshal Montgomery addressed the division as they were been disbanded as they were no longer needed due to the surrender of the Germans, this is a quote of his words at that time from the original booklet.
  Guards Armoured Division
  "Farewell To Armour Parade" Rotenburg Airfield Germany
  9th June 1945

Address by Field Marshal Montgomery to the Guards Division;

1. The Field-Marshal began by saying that the German war being over, it was nteresting to consider how it was that we had won when in 1940 and in 1941 and even in 1942 it had seemed quite impossible that we shourl ever win. There were many reasons for this, but he always considered that there were two reasons which were basically the main cause of the enemys defeat.

   Firstly, the great mistakes made by the enemy beginning in 1941 when the Germans attacked Russia and Japan attacked the Americans, thus bringing these two great nations in on our side.

   Secondly, the good fighting qualities of the Allied soldiers whom the fighting man of the British Empire stands out in proud position.

2. The Field-Marshal then went on to speak as follows; -

   "And now I want to say something about your Division.

   When the war began the Guards were infantry.

   At a time of great national danger in 1941 the guards formed armoured formations. The Guards Armoured Division and the 6 Guards Armoured Brigade fought throughout this historic campaign in western Europe.

   I don;t suppose there is any officer in the Army who can speak with such weight of experience as myself about the relative standards of battle efficiency of this or that formation of unit.

   From Alamein to the Baltic, I have had many formations and units under my command.

   I want to say, here and now, that un the sphere of armoured warfare the Guards have seta standarad that it will be difficult for those that come after to reach.

   In modern war it is the cooperation of all arms

armoured and un-armoured, that wins the battle, and in this respect you have achieved great results. In fact, the Guards have shown that whatever they are asked to do, what ever they take on, they do well: maintaining always the highest standards and giving a lead to all others. You will long be remembered for you prowess in armoured war.

And now you are to return to your traditional role of infantry. Some of you may wonder why this is so. There are many reasons. First: The King wishes it. Second; the Brigade of Guards as a while are anxious that this should be done. And Third: I myself, an infantry soldier of many years service, would say to you that you are needed as infantry, the infantry arm has come right to the fore in this war; it is the most versatile of all the arms; nothing can be done without infantry to help; there is never enough infantry for the tasks that have to be done.

It is vital that the infantry of the British Army should be a firm and strong rock on which to build the post war Army. It is the central core of the fighting machine, on which all else depends.

We need you in the infantry; we need your high standards, your great efficiency in all matters, and your old traditions of duty and service; all these are needed to help weld the infantry arm into a firm and solid basis on which to build.

And so I welcome you back into the infantry.

You can look back with pride on your excursion into the realms of armoured warfare; and the experience there gained will always be valuable to you.

Then we went onto Cologne and on Guard, after we'd done that we moved near Hamburg into all the farming villages, we were holding the land sort of thing where the occupation were. We moved to the different farming villas because they thought that there might have been an underground movement called the Werewolf, but it never transpired so for a period we'd rest and relaxation. We were allocated our occupation area which was Cologne which the Americans had taken, we moved down in convoy on to the outskirts of Cologne and after a long move we took up residence in Cologne and had a lot of Guard Duties, they'd commandeered the civilian houses and what not told the civilians,

'Out, soldiers are staying here.' all with furniture and what not.

There was a displaced persons camp for the Russians forced labour people, and there was a camp for the Polish y'know, the people who had been used for forced labour. Now then that was a bad sight to see when the Russians were been taken back, they knew that life was finished for them because they had worked for the Germans even though they had been forced as compulsory like. It was a Russian prisoner of war camp, they stood at the wire, we couldn't do anything for them, this was up in the area which was a horrible area, and I can't remember the name.

'There were four camps in Munster, near Cologne where Grandad was, research suggests that he is talking about Camp Munster IV, which was specifically reserved for Russian prisoners.'

There was this here barbed wire fence and they were scavenging I don't know what happened to them I suppose people would come up and feed them like, it was a pitiful site to see them like this. We use to take them back up to the Russian zone area and we used to have to put armed escorts with them so they wouldn't escape you see, I do believe thousands of Russians, because they'd worked in Germany were exterminated when they got back to Russia. Well they were seen as traitors like even though they hadn't fought and they had been forced into labour like, so that's why a lot of Russian and Polish people tried to escape and come to England or where ever. It was an evil regime was communism; unless you were 'up' in the communists it was a poor life for you. They were sent to the Stallag's or what ever they call them, that were a sad job to do that and fortunately I was never sent to do that job.

So we were there and we use to do Guard Duty, there was only one bridge a big timber bridge across the Rhine and as you crossed over it there was Cologne Cathedral on your left hand side, all around the streets you would go down there was just rubble y'know, just heaps of rubble all the way around. Everything was battered y'know I mean you'd drive down a street, a road and everything around ya was rubble y'know like it was total devastation.

So we use to do a Guard on the river bridge, I did quite a number of Guards there; one particular the Rhine Bridge was an interesting one because we'd both sides of the bridge with sentries on, the train would come over to one side and then they'd transport to the other side. Well the people were going out of the city into the countryside for food and they'd come back and you'd have to escort them back across the bridge y'see. There was a power station too, there was a wine warehouse, I never got bloody lucky to land that one and there was a slaughter place, an abattoir, I dropped on all of them but I never got the bloody wine warehouse.

Top left: Beryl May Clough and Steve circa April / May 1945 in England.

Top right: Cpt. Ian Oswald Liddell V.C Taken from the newspaper article (Times) in his file at the Regimental HQ Archives.

Above: Captain Ian Oswald Liddell VC Courtesy of Regimental HQ Wellington Barracks.

Left: Cpt Ian Oswald Liddell V.C Taken from the newspaper article in his file at the Regimental HQ Archives.

Stephen Simpson
Peacock
Horace Camm
Freddy Dent

Facing page top: The bridge Cpt Liddell disarmed. Photograph courtesy of Regimental HQ Wellington Barracks.

Facing page middle: Photograph taken of the remaining Carrier Platoon, 1945 before they were disbanded. 8 in from left at back Steve, 3 in from left at front Peacock and 5 in from left at front is Horace Camm.

Facing page bottom: A Guards Armoured tank crossing the bridge Cpt Liddell disarmed. Photograph courtesy of Regimental HQ Wellington Barracks.

Steve's original 3rd Battalion shoulder cloth badges unpicked from his uniform.

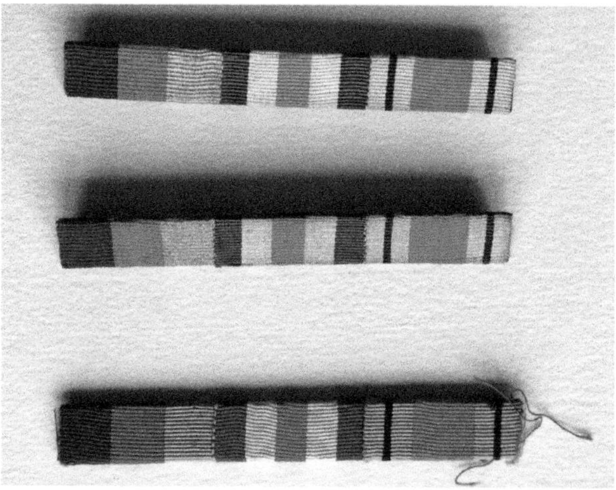

Steve's pin stripes that would be pinned to his uniform to illustrate campaigns he has taken part in. 1939-1945 Star, France & Germany Star, Defence Medal, War Medal 1939 – 1945, General Service Medal Palestine 1945 – 1948.

Facing page top: Original 1 and 5 Mark allied military currency bank notes dated 1944.

Above: German surrender

Right: This is the original booklet front cover containing Field Marshal Montgomery's speech to the soldiers.

Facing page bottom: A page from Steve's Soldiers Service Book with a sticker covering an area, stamped by Orderly Room 3rd Battalion

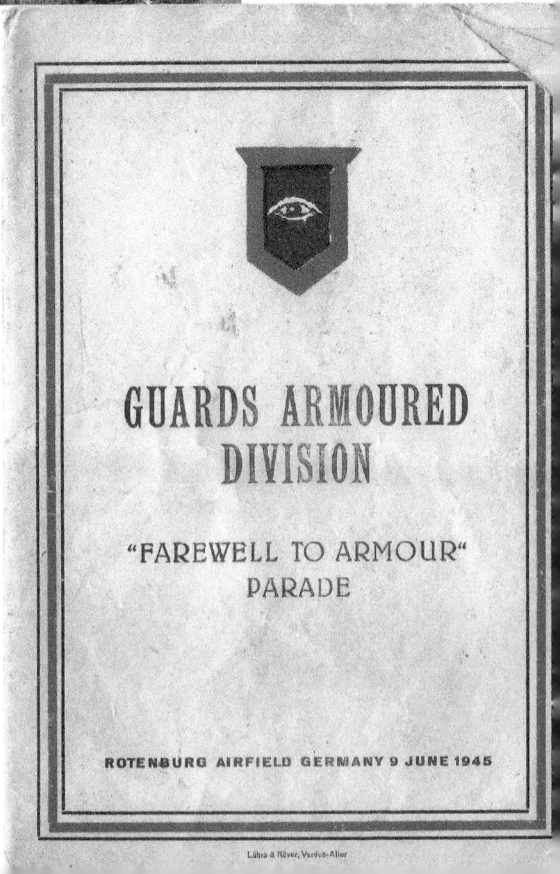

GUARDS ARMOURED DIVISION

"FAREWELL TO ARMOUR" PARADE

ROTENBURG AIRFIELD GERMANY 9 JUNE 1945

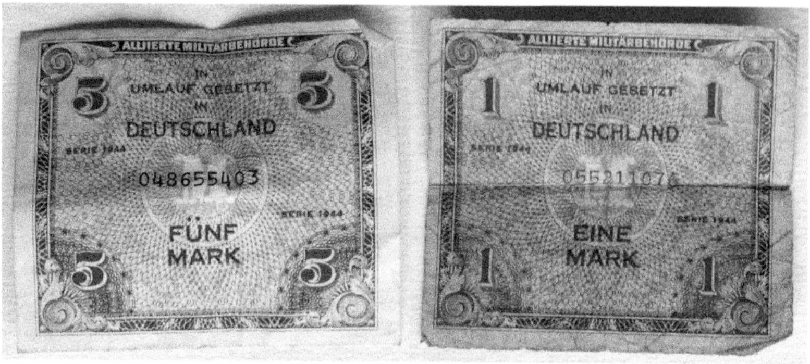

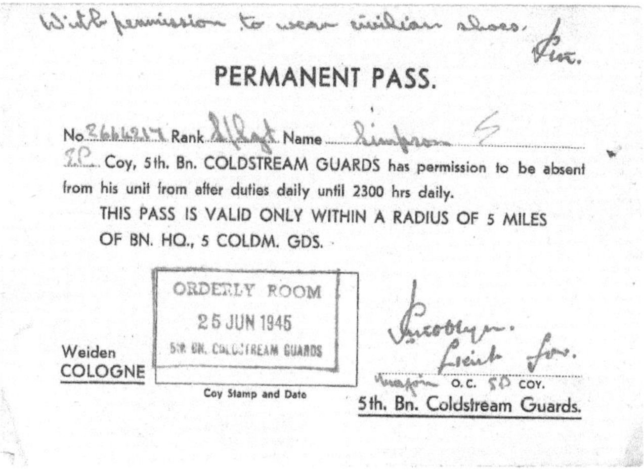
With permission to wear civilian shoes.

PERMANENT PASS.

No. 2664217 Rank L/Sgt Name Simpson

S.P. Coy, 5th. Bn. COLDSTREAM GUARDS has permission to be absent from his unit from after duties daily until 2300 hrs daily.

THIS PASS IS VALID ONLY WITHIN A RADIUS OF 5 MILES OF BN. HQ., 5 COLDM. GDS.

ORDERLY ROOM
25 JUN 1945
5th BN. COLDSTREAM GUARDS

Coy Stamp and Date

Weiden
COLOGNE

Lieut for.
Major O.C. S.P. COY.
5th. Bn. Coldstream Guards.

Above: Pass out for Cologne dated 25th June 1945, kept for all these years with his collection. The handwriting at the top reads; With permission to wear civilian shoes.

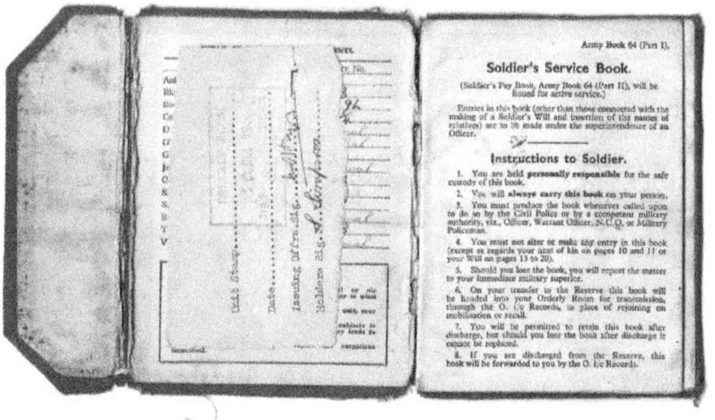

Above: The news articles reporting the Farwell to Armour Parade and The Times article on the Coldstream Guards Actions, plus a copy of a map of the 5th Battalions movements across Europe.

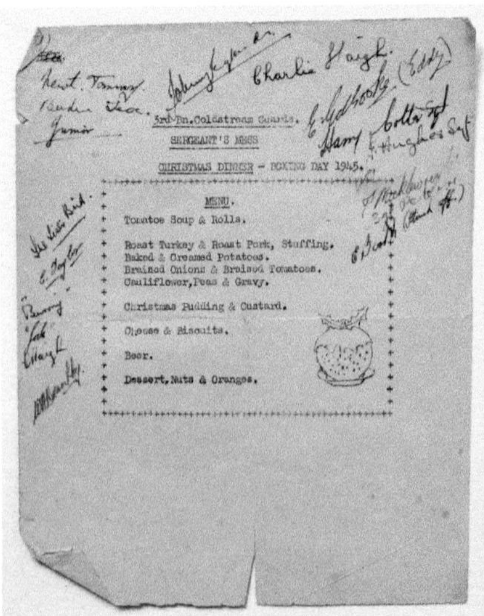

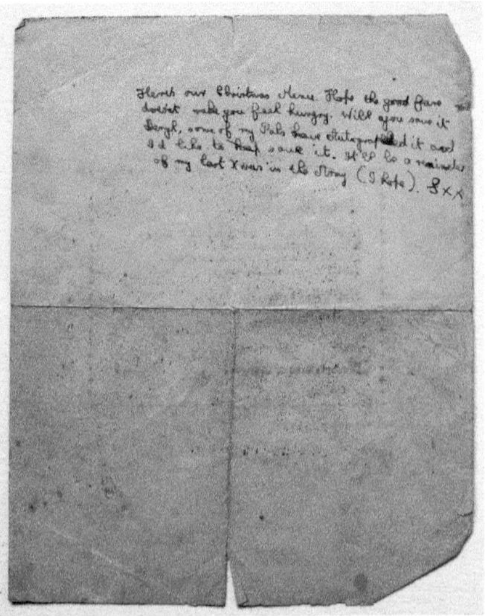

Below: Left of picture War Diary, Soldiers Service & Pay Book, Photo of Steve and original enlistment invitation to recruit. Front centre, May's envelope containing her letter to Steve, top centre original Brussels Sprout. Right of picture original form for recruiting Steve, original red Regular Army Certificate of Service book, original soldiers release book. Central photograph of 13th Squadron Sgt Boxer Browns Squad 1941.

Facing page bottom: The original Boxing Day menu from 1945, Steve got his comrades to autograph the menu and he wrote on the back and posted it home to Beryl, it reads;

Here's our Christmas menu, hope the good fare doesn't make you feel hungry. Will you save it Beryl, some of my pal's have autographed it and I'd like to save it. It'll be a reminder of my last Xmas in the Army. (I hope). S xxx

8

'WHILST SHEPARD'S WATCH!'

At the end I was thinking I want to get home as soon as I can now, I wasn't feared of anymore fighting, that's over and done with, your nerves were still a bit stretched if you know what I mean and so I volunteered for the Far East thinking now our jobs done I shall get home to England and that'll be it, bloody Jap war will finish and there'll be no need for us and I shall be at home for Beryl like y'see, that was my thinking.

'Around this time Beryl's mother May wrote a lengthy letter to Steve outlining plans for his return home with her daughter, the letter reads as follow;'

Dear Steve,

I received your letter yesterday and Beryl also had one, which she answered last night, and I cannot understand you saying you have not had a letter from her as I know she has written every week lately and your letters to her are nearly always about 12-14 days, between the pair of you, you worry me to death and I shall be very glad when you both meet again, do you know Steve when those two letters came yesterday I felt quite upset and I know I shouldn't and when Beryl tells me not to worry I still can't help it, you are both waiting for one another and yet you each keep the other waiting for letters, every day Beryl comes in, 'any mail Mam?' you write to me ask Beryl to write, you're an awful pair, so can you wander that I shall be glad when you both get together again, I don't suppose I'd take any notice only I am still taking a lot of drugs and it makes me look on the wrong side of things.

'(May had been burned in a terrible accident when her caravan blew up whilst she was in it on holiday with her husband George. She was a small framed woman anyway and the burns were severe and scarred her for the rest of her life all over her body and face.)'

Well Steve I'll bet you are making the most of your time now as you will soon be home, and don't forget to let us know the minute you land, as bad as you are we are looking forward to seeing you, then I'll tell you if I think you're handsome as well as smart, you know best I have to scold now and then because I treat you as part of my family.

Did you know Ruby and Gordon have gone to Cornwall for a fortnight so I have Ros and Anne here, Malcolm is running at Roundhay on children's day, (Sat) and he is 14 on Thursday July 11th so he is going to have a little party before the bread rationing starts, just imagining Steve when you come to us you'll have to carry your bread ration don't you think its awful. Well I don't you can have that job with us, as you told us to concrete all the garden and we haven't enough petrol to run the car very much, so I think you'll have to be a handyman and help indoors as well, you told Beryl about Bill going in the police and she told me, well for a change we have had a lovely and we picked a big dish full of strawberries and cream for dessert. Well Steve dear it is 9pm and George has just come in so I will have to finish this letter.

By the way we had a wedding in our street last Thursday and Iris and Walt have come back off their holiday and Owens have come back off theirs and we start ours, that is George, Malcolm, I, Ruby, Ros and Anne on July 20th and you'll be on your way home then and I hope you wont be too disappointed with life in England.

Well dear I am tired and so will close with love from all.

Your Loving Mother xxx

P.S this is some of the writing paper Beryl bought for me

The idea was our 3rd Battalion, all soldiers like myself who were coming back to England, we were going to go to Kentucky and train with the American Rangers and we were going to be the assault soldiers on Singapore. We were drafted back to England and we landed down, I think it was Folkstone and they took us on a train all the way bloody up to Scotland and 3rd Battalion were reforming again and so they paid us out and then the following day they sent us on leave. So I was thinking,

'Well this is me then, 3rd Battalion in England filling my time in until I'm demobbed.'

Anyway it turned out that the plans were that the 3rd Battalion were going to go to Kentucky and we were going to train with the American Rangers this is what we were told the plans were, then we were going to be the assault parade on Singapore so that'd of been a shit of a job y'know. So fortunately for me the old Yankee Doodles dropped their egg on Nagasaki and it was over, that was it, so I finished my time in Palestine, trouble had started in Palestine you know with the Jews outta Germany wanting to get to their homelands, so the Arabs were kicking up and the Jews were kicking up so we were sent there as peace keepers like sort of thing.

I wish now I'd made more use of my time roaming it but I suppose we were restricted in a way with troubles been on there like y'know, I would have loved to have done more. I did go out with the Padre one Easter and we went round Capernaum and the Sea of Galilee and Tiberias and he took us to a place where it said in the bible Jesus spoke to the multitude at Galilee and it was sort of like a bay and it was rising up and the Padre said to me,

'You go down there.' and then he talked and I could hear him as clear as crystal y'know and you could understand Jesus speaking to the multitude at Capernaum like.

I went to a Church of England school and I was brought up Cof E like and I'm not a believer or a disbeliever, there are some things you thought of as a child or you can read in the bible, While Sheppard's watched! Now then I remembered this particular Christmas Eve, it was a still calm cool night, bloody massive stars in the sky there and you could hear sheep, or the goats on the land bleating and they were, while Sheppard's watched their flocks y'know like, and I thought well it isn't far out isn't that. I'd have thought it's a sort of Grimm's Fairytale y'know is the bible, but no, some things they make you think, I mean, as I say that particular incidence, that particular night, Christmas Eve, big stars, cool and crisp, the sheep bleating, the Sheppard's watching y'know. When I was in trouble and there were shit flying round me I thought well I never prayed before, surely it's an un-honourable thing to pray now cos I'm in trouble!

⋆

I had leave a couple of times whilst there, I went to Beruit and had some good food and beach bathing and drinking like y'know, eventually when my Demob Number came up we went training and we crossed the Sinai Desert we finished up in Egypt at a place called Sidi Bishr at a Transit Camp, we held there for a week, coming back from Palestine I boarded a train and I've still got marks on my arse from the boards to this day.

Well we left Palestine we went by train and a dear friend of mine Johnny England, we were Sergeants together in't platoon, we served together for a long, long time and we used to get pissed together me and old John. We'd happy times together we used to share the bunk and we travelled together to a place called Sidi Bishr by train through Sinai.

There was a transit camp at one side of the road and opposite was a leave camp called the Lone Palm, Lone Palm Leave Camp, it was only for lads that were on leave who could use its facilities. So there was a Coldstream Officer on staff there so Johnny and I approached him and said,

'Is there any chance of getting a permit here to use the facilities Sir?'

'I'll see the Governor.'

So anyway we got a little Chitty, I've still got it amongst my souvenirs, so we got a little chitty to use the Lone Palm Leave Camp, well there were a lovely bar there y'know and there were WVS ladies working there and one played the piano, well silly bugger me when I've had a jar or two I like to sing.

'Grandad started singing 'We've got the lilacs in the spring again.'

Well she thought I was the bees knees this here woman y'know and they'd bring the fillies in from Alexandria and they'd say,

'Oh you don't want to be with those girls, not nice those ladies.'

Anyway me and old Johnno we used to get pissed and stagger out of the camp and oh the Lone Farm Leave, I bet that buggers collapsed now. We had our own private beach and as I say we'd had a skip full this particular night and we went down on the beach with the sun shades like and deck chairs, just little shorts on like y'see, really got central and the sun came round, well I was like a lobster I were burnt, right away I could peel bloody skin and peel it off right away, ooh I was in bloody agony.

Dated 3rd July 1946 addressed to Steve in the 3rd Battalion this is the envelope containing the original letter from May, Steve's Mother-in-law to be.

After a week we got a ship from Alexandria to Tolong, Palestine, and then we travelled by train then, this was evening time and then all night on the train and then the train stopped for you to have a wash and what not and have a meal and then carried on all day and all night and then next morning you landed at Calais. Then boat over to England then we boarded the train for all night, all day, all night and all day to Calais, my arse looked like the lattice boards we were sat on. From there we got the ferry to England to Aldershot and demobbed, that was the end of my soldiering career, I left the regiment in the August of 1946 and my time expired, I was on leave until November, I'd 3 months leave like y'see, which I'd accrued, until November and from then on I was on reserve like y'see. I didn't have a job to go to, I used to meet up with my mucka Reggie Baker and my Dad used to say,

'Where you been all week?' once I got home.

I will add a comment; Now they are calling them heroes, then they were heroes, to my mind everyone was worthy of a V.C particularly the Infantry lads.

Original Republique Syrienne 25 Piastres bank note
dated 19th April 1942

Steve, taken in Palestine circa 1946

Taken in Palestine circa 1946 on the back of this photograph Steve had written; 'Two Garforth Lads.' The village where Steve was from back in Yorkshire.

Taken in Palestine 1946 Steve is 3rd from left.

Left John England and
Steve right, taken in
Palestine 1946.

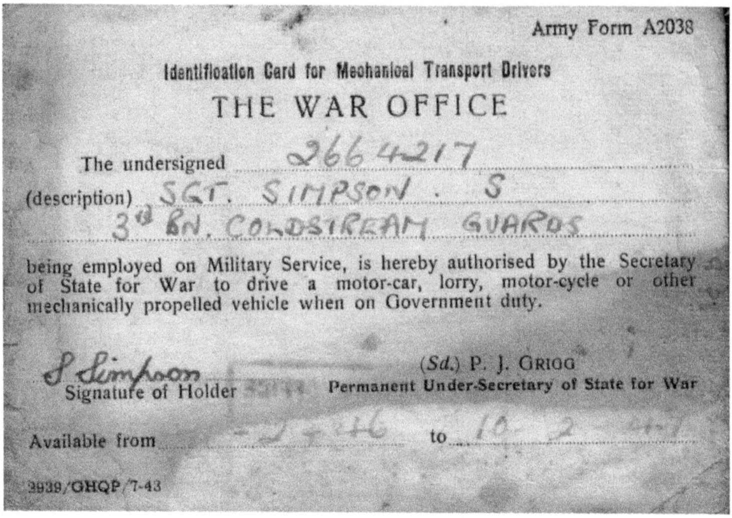
Army Form A2038

Identification Card for Mechanical Transport Drivers

THE WAR OFFICE

The undersigned 2664217

(description) SGT. SIMPSON . S
3rd BN. COLDSTREAM GUARDS

being employed on Military Service, is hereby authorised by the Secretary of State for War to drive a motor-car, lorry, motor-cycle or other mechanically propelled vehicle when on Government duty.

S Simpson
Signature of Holder

(Sd.) P. J. GRIGG
Permanent Under-Secretary of State for War

Available from -2-46 to 10-2-47

3939/GHQP/7-43

Steve's Vehicle License issued whilst in Palestine where he drove Field Marshal Montgomery's around for a short while.

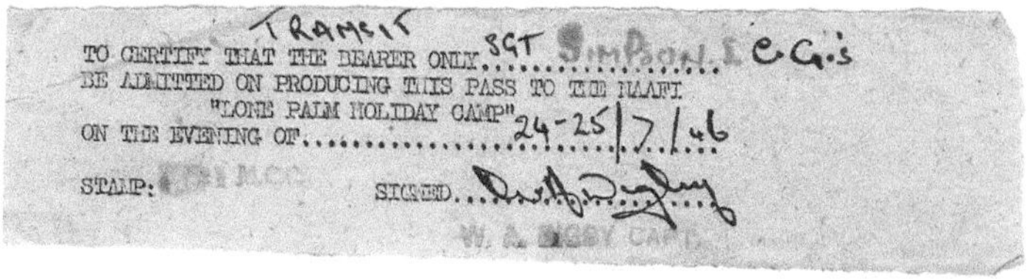
TRANSIT

TO CERTIFY THAT THE BEARER ONLY SGT SIMPSON. S C.G.'s
BE ADMITTED ON PRODUCING THIS PASS TO THE NAAFI
"LONE PALM HOLIDAY CAMP" 24-25/7/46
ON THE EVENING OF

STAMP: SIGNED

The original Chitty for Lone Palm Holiday Camp, Steve kept even the smallest of bits of paper to mark his amazing journey.

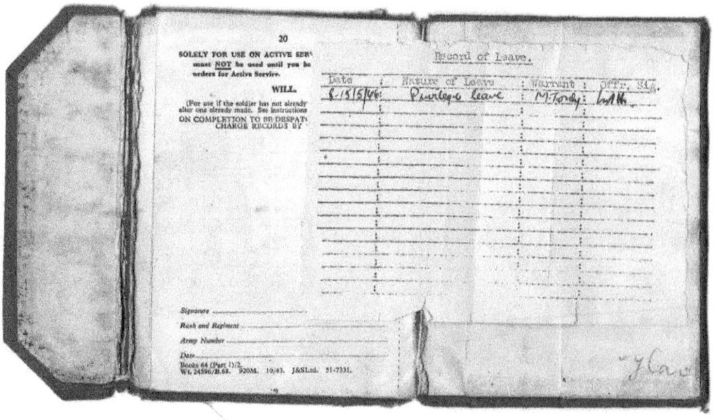
20

SOLELY FOR USE ON ACTIVE SER
must NOT be used until you be
orders for Active Service.

WILL.

Record of Leave.

Date	Nature of Leave	Warrant	Offr. Sig.
8-15/5/46	Privilege Leave	M.T.only	

This page of his Soldiers Service Book shows Privilege Leave was given to him 8 – 15th May 1946 which would have been for Palestine.

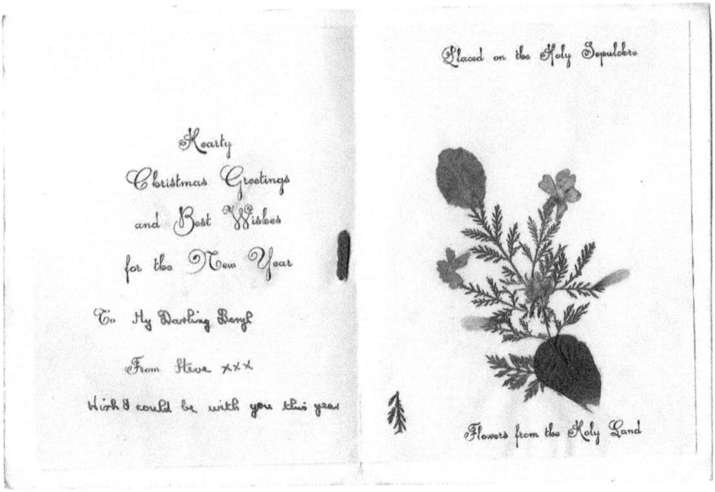

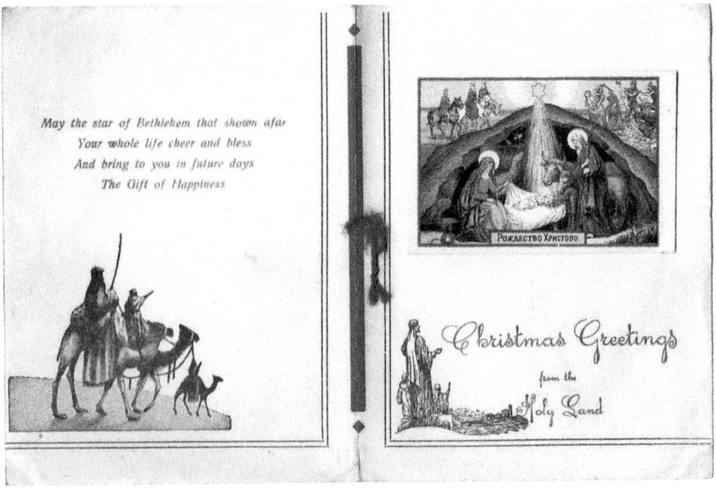

A Christmas card sent to Beryl from Steve
from the holy land. It reads;
'To my darling Beryl, from Steve. Wish I could be
with you this year. Xxx'

Left Ralph Revell, (served in the RAF he married Beryl's cousin) right Steve, taken on Blackpool Promenade 1946 during leave.

9

'WHEN I HAVE A LITTLE GIRL...'

I have made the pilgrimage over on the 40th Anniversary and I was fortunate to be able to visit my friends in Belgium, it was lovely to see them again, in fact when I visited it, this 'ere Neerheylissem the lady there, I was 21 at the time, the lady of the house would have been 30ish and the old grandmother she and her husband Louis, Millie they called the lady, Tom and I shared a bedroom, we shared a bed. They had this little girl they called Jannine she was what, four or five years old, she used to sit on me knee, I tried to talk a little French, used to call her La Belle Mademoiselle from Bruxelle, y'know and things like that to her, I said to her,

'When I have a little girl I'm gonna call her Jannine' and she beamed, they were very nice people.

So I went back with my son Stephen we went over for the 40th anniversary and called to see them, we pulled into the street and our Stephen said,

'You won't know which house it is Dad' and I said

'Now then the only thing which has altered here is this 'ere road, it were cobbled before and they were gonna tarmac it' I said 'and that's the bedroom I was in up there.'

So I went and knocked on the door and this old lady of 70 odd came to the door.

'Madame Cachard?' I enquired.

'Oui' she said and then,

'Steve' I said '…Steve, Steve.'

'Steve?' she said, it hadn't clicked and I had a photograph of myself from that time and I showed her it.

'AHHHHH Steve!' she cried, 'come in, come in.' So bloody brandy bottle came out and she gets on't phone, I heard her say,

'Tout de suite.'

Well within minutes bloody door bangs open and this here Jannine comes bounding in, a lass of 45 and her husband Andre. Oh and we finished up, it was a fantastic night, as I say we went into a place called Tirlemont for the evening and we had a right bleeding feast, numerous beers and what not, I said to André,

'It's our treat, we will pay for this cos we…'

'No, no, you stay with us tonight, we pay for meal, it is all taken care of.' he says.

We had a bloody slap up meal and the lot, so we gets in the car after, I had a Volvo at the time, we gets in the car on us way back and I say,

'Left turn?'

'No turn right' he said.

'Turn right?'

Well we goes in to this little estaminet, well all their friends were in there, bloody beer coming in from all over, so we were having a right time me and old Steve, when they all started piling out they said,

'You come'

Well we ended up at a nightclub way out in the country y'know and they were bloody boozing and dancing, tee hee, I didn't tell your Nana that like, it was lovely, they really are lovely people.

Then my son Stephen and I we went down to Arromanches and took part in the D-Day celebration, one I'll never forget. I visited the cemetery where my cousin is buried Clifford

Wilkinson he was with the Wiltshire Regiment and I visited the cemetery where my three comrades were buried. After that I then went over for the 50th Anniversary and Jack Camidge and I went over on 55th year and did our pilgrimage again and paid our respects. Hopefully God been willing we shall be attending on the 60th anniversary, so I will let you know my thoughts and feelings then.

Normandy, when we see it now and think of the times when we first saw it, it is lovely now, everything was battered and shattered and smelt, now its lovely green fields and so on, some places I tried to visit but I couldn't trace them like.

I brought back a number of souvenirs from my time, I collared two German lads, Paratroopers and disarmed them I cleared them and I got ones compass and one his Swiss Army Knife, I gave it to Malcolm my brother in law and a bayonet, I gave that to my nephew's lad and Charles my grandson, he has the compass.

That was a sad job I forgot to tell ya, I collared these two lads one time it was a little incident at the time of the closing of the Falaise Gap, our division had been squeezed out of the action itself and the Canadians and Americans had pinched in. So my section, we were sent out on a standing patrol in front of the Battalion, we were down this here track and it were all overgrown over it. I come to this corner and this battered farmhouse and there was countryside out in front of it y'see, you could see the German ambulances crossing over the front like. I'd go out first light and I'd stay there all day, then pull back into Battalion area at night time, well I was in the farmhouse it was all broke down and I was doing something, I heard somebody shouting,

'Hande hoch, Hande hoch!'

Horace's bloody Bren gun, it was stuck and he couldn't get it to fire off and there were two German lads approaching so I nipped round the corner and collared them both and disarmed them, to make sure they had no grenades on 'em like. Well they were two lads probably about 18 or 19 years old y'know, there was no fighting them, they must have been left behind and they were trying to work their way through, so we sent 'em back up to the Battalion Head Quarters, unfortunately when they got back there, Battalion Head Quarters was shelled and these two lads were killed. It was sad was that I mean I never came into close contact Bayonet wise with 'em like y'see more often than not you were at a distance when you were firing y'know, you'd see 'em and you'd either grenade 'em or mortar them or shoot at 'em like. You'd see 'em go down aye and they might of just gone down, they might have been wounded, you just don't know, I like to think I only just wounded 'em like y'know.

I suppose it must have changed the way I lived my life, I have a feeling for people if they're in trouble y'know, I sympathise with them and if I can help anybody I will do y'know, I think that's the thing it did for me, I was helped a lot and if I can help anybody like wise I will. Some you can take with a pinch of salt like, but by enlarge everybody's ok until they do something different, I take everybody on trust sort of thing and I value friendship, I value the friendship of my old comrade's y'know, I value the friendship of the younger Regiment, I value their friendship and it's true what they say, that it's a Coldstream family and I find it is so, it is aye. There's a feeling that no matter where you go in this world if you see this fella with the Brigade Tie on and they say,

'What Regiment were ya pal?' and you say,

'Coldstream.'

Then you have got a mate, it don't matter if you're in Timbuktu, you've got a friend.

'Grandad started to get upset again at how this made him feel, that sense of belonging and friendship was valud greatly by him.'

Well that's about it from me as I say and I am looking forward to my returning on the 60th I shall be going to see my three mates graves, and pay my respects again.

'Grandad started to cry at the ever fresh memory of their loss'

Aye you think of folks, one lad I use to see from my Carrier Crew there was Horace he was me Bren gunner, then there were young Peter he was a, well I used to shout at him, I used to shout at Peacock, I use to kick his arse on y'know. He was one where a shell would land and he was all jittery and I use to say,

'Come on, get on with ya, get ya bloody cig going, your alright I'm with ya. Dig a bloody hole and get in it.'

I'd have a go like y'know.

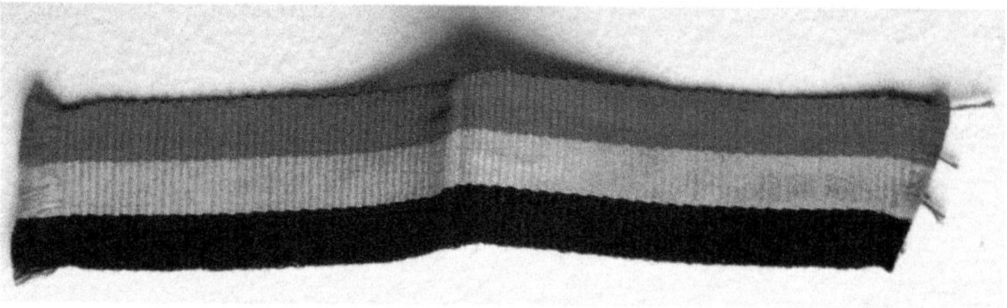

German stripes amongst Steve's collection,
taken from the two lads he captured and disarmed.

A WWI German cross found amongst Steve's collection,
from the two lads he captured and disarmed.

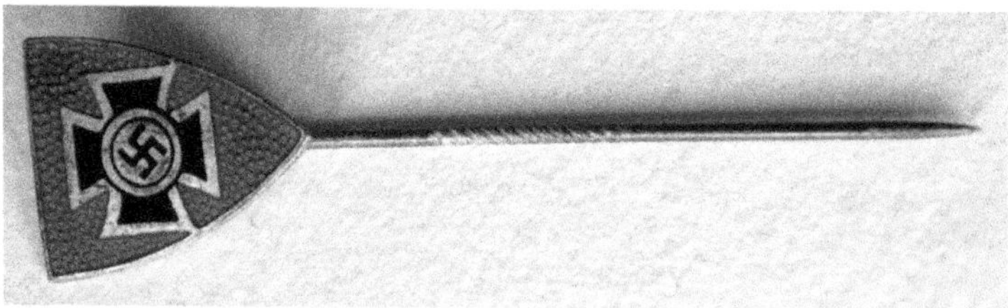

A German pin from the two lads he captured and disarmed.

A German stamp from Steve's
collection.

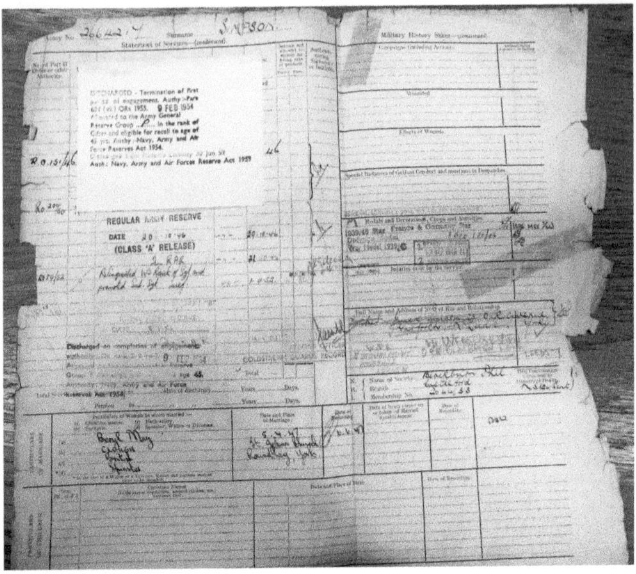

REGULAR ARMY RESERVE

(CLASS 'A' RELEASE)

Above: Photograph of Steve's Military History sheet taken from his Records at the Archives, Wellington Barracks 2015. The document has been stamped with his official release from the army and allocated to the army reserve until the age of 45. It also says; Relinquished W/S Rank of Sgt and promoted Sub Sgt
It states his wife as Beryl Clough married 5th April 1947 and describes his Medals and Decorations as; 1939/45 Star France & Germany Star, Defence Medal, War Medal 1939/45. Stamped as given 22nd September 1948.

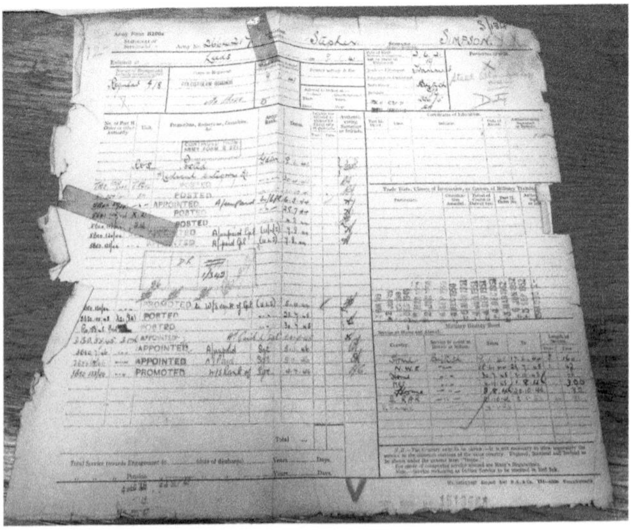

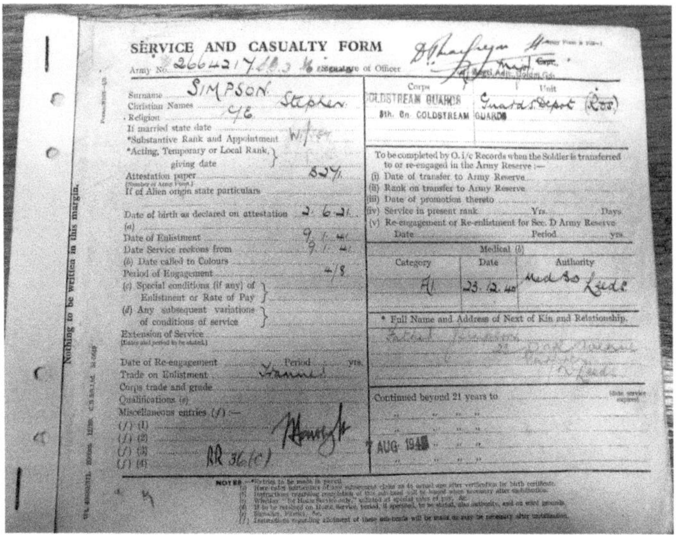

SERVICE AND CASUALTY FORM

Army No. 2664217 ... Signature of Officer

Surname SIMPSON
Christian Names Stephen
Religion C.E.
If married state date
*Substantive Rank and Appointment W/S
*Acting, Temporary or Local Rank, giving date
Attestation paper 824
If of Alien origin state particulars
Date of birth as declared on attestation 2.6.21
Date of Enlistment 9.1.41
Date Service reckons from 9.1.41
(b) Date called to Colours
Period of Engagement 4/8
(c) Special conditions (if any) of Enlistment or Rate of Pay
(d) Any subsequent variations of conditions of service
Extension of Service
Date of Re-engagement ... Period ... yrs.
Trade on Enlistment Tanner
Corps trade and grade
Qualifications (e)
Miscellaneous entries (f) —
AR 36(C)

Corps: COLDSTREAM GUARDS; 5th. Bn. COLDSTREAM GUARDS
Unit: Guards Depot (RDS)

To be completed by O. i/c Records when the Soldier is transferred to or re-engaged in the Army Reserve:—
(i) Date of transfer to Army Reserve
(ii) Rank on transfer to Army Reserve
(iii) Date of promotion thereto
(iv) Service in present rank ... Yrs. ... Days
(v) Re-engagement or Re-enlistment for Sec. D Army Reserve Date ... Period ... yrs.

Medical (f)

Category	Date	Authority
A1	23.12.40	Med Bo Leeds

* Full Name and Address of Next of Kin and Relationship.

Continued beyond 21 years to

AUG 1945

Above: Photograph taken of Steve's Service and Casualty Form at Wellington Barracks Archives 2015 giving his basic information of service number 2664217 5th Battalion Coldstream Guards date of birth at attestation etc

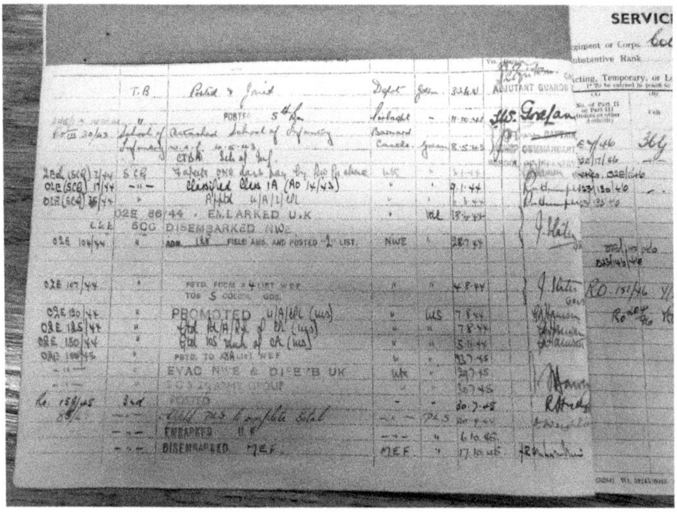

SERVICE
Regiment or Corps Col
Substantive Rank
Acting, Temporary, or L
ADJUTANT GUARDS
T.B. Posted & Joins
POSTED 5th Bn
Pirbright
Barnard Castle
EMBARKED U.K.
DISEMBARKED NWE
NWE
PROMOTED
EVAC NWE & DISEMB UK
POSTED
EMBARKED U.K.
DISEMBARKED MEF
MEF

Above: Dates listed of Emabrking and Disembarking and where including Pirbright and North West Europe.

Bottom facing page: Photograph taken at Regimental Archives of Steve's Military Service Sheet/War Records. It lists his promotions and posts with dates, his age at enlistment 19, the first entry Unit RDS Posted Gdsm 9.1.41 to Promoted to W/S Rank of Sgt 4.7.46

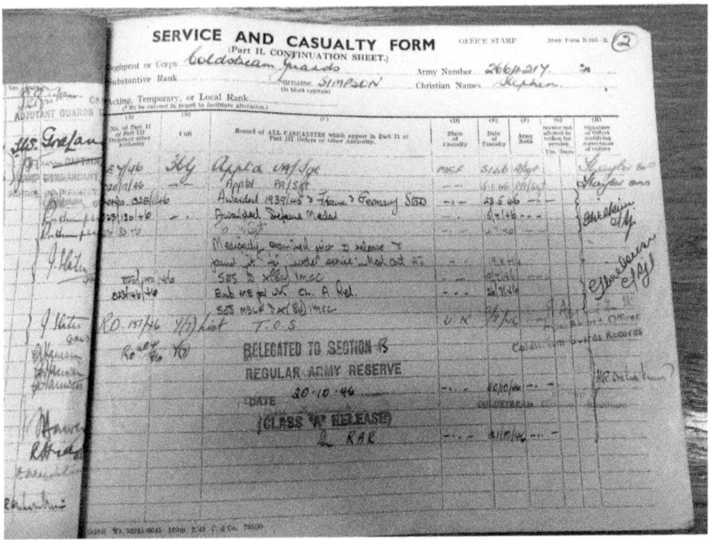

SERVICE AND CASUALTY FORM
(Part II. CONTINUATION SHEET.)

Regiment or Corps: Coldstream Guards
Substantive Rank
Surname: SIMPSON
Army Number: 2664217
Christian Names: Stephen
Acting, Temporary, or Local Rank

RELEGATED TO SECTION B
REGULAR ARMY RESERVE
DATE 20.10.46
(CLASS "A" RELEASE)

Steve's Service and Casualty Form, listing his awards/medals and his medical on release as Fit and that he was regulated to regular army reserve.

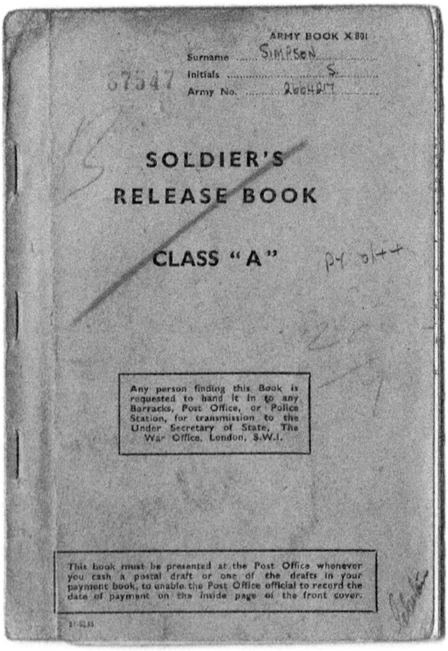

ARMY BOOK X 801
Surname: SIMPSON
Initials: S.
Army No.: 2664217

SOLDIER'S
RELEASE BOOK
CLASS "A"

Any person finding this Book is requested to hand it in to any Barracks, Post Office, or Police Station, for transmission to the Under Secretary of State, The War Office, London, S.W.1.

This book must be presented at the Post Office whenever you cash a postal draft or one of the drafts in your payment book, to enable the Post Office official to record the date of payment on the inside page of the front cover.

Steve's original Soldiers Release Book.

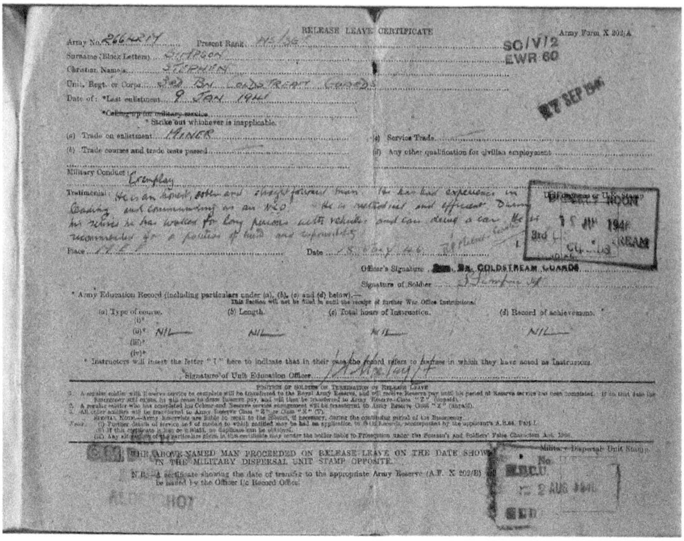

RELEASE LEAVE CERTIFICATE

Army Form X 202/A

Army No. 2664214 Present Rank L/Sgt

SC/V/2
EWR 60

Surname (Block Letters) SIMPSON

Christian Name/s STEPHEN

Unit, Regt. or Corps 3rd Bn Coldstream Guards

Date of: *Last enlistment 9 JAN 1941

~~*Calling up for military service~~

* Strike out whichever is inapplicable.

(a) Trade on enlistment MINER

(b) Trade courses and trade tests passed

(c) Service Trade

(d) Any other qualification for civilian employment

Military Conduct: Exemplary

Testimonial: He is an honest, sober and straight forward man. He has had experience in leading and commanding as an NCO. He is methodical and efficient. During his service he has worked for long periods with vehicles and can drive a car. He is recommended for a position of trust and responsibility.

Place [illegible] Date 18 July 46

Officer's Signature ... Bn. COLDSTREAM GUARDS

Signature of Soldier [illegible]

* Army Education Record (including particulars under (a), (b), (c) and (d) below).—
This Section will not be filled in until the receipt of further War Office Instructions.

(a) Type of course.	(b) Length.	(c) Total hours of Instruction.	(d) Record of achievement.
(i)*			
(ii)* NIL	NIL	NIL	NIL
(iii)*			
(iv)*			

* Instructors will insert the letter "I" here to indicate that in their case the record refers to courses in which they have acted as Instructors.

Signature of Unit Education Officer [illegible]

POSITION OF SOLDIER ON TERMINATION OF RELEASE LEAVE

[illegible]

THE ABOVE NAMED MAN PROCEEDED ON RELEASE LEAVE ON THE DATE SHOWN IN THE MILITARY DISPERSAL UNIT STAMP OPPOSITE.

N.B.—A certificate showing the date of transfer to the appropriate Army Reserve (A.F. X 202/B) will be issued by the Officer i/c Record Office.

Military Dispersal Unit Stamp

2 AUG 1946

This is the reference in Steve's Release Book;

He is an honest, sober and straight forward man. He has had experiences in leading and commanding as an N.C.O. He is methodical and efficient. During his service he has worked for long periods with vehicles and can drive a car. He is recommended for a position of trust and responsibility.

Steve's original Regular Army, Certificate of Service book.

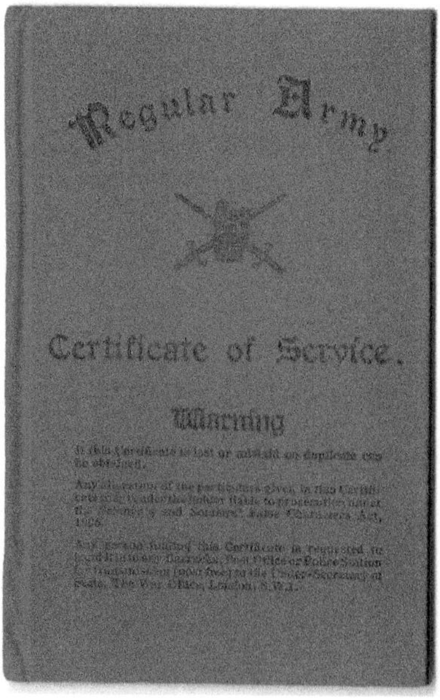

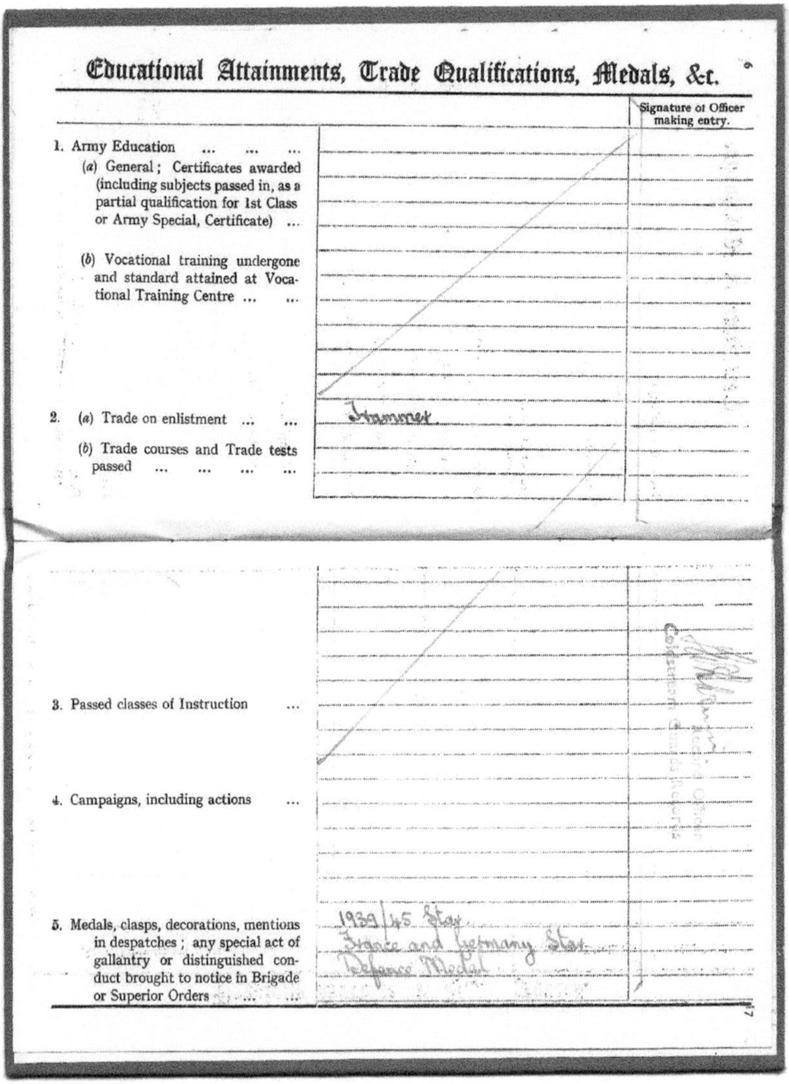

Educational Attainments, Trade Qualifications, Medals, &c.

		Signature of Officer making entry.
1. Army Education		
(a) General; Certificates awarded (including subjects passed in, as a partial qualification for 1st Class or Army Special, Certificate) ...		
(b) Vocational training undergone and standard attained at Vocational Training Centre		
2. (a) Trade on enlistment	Hammer	
(b) Trade courses and Trade tests passed		
3. Passed classes of Instruction ...		
4. Campaigns, including actions ...		
5. Medals, clasps, decorations, mentions in despatches; any special act of gallantry or distinguished conduct brought to notice in Brigade or Superior Orders	1939/45 Star France and Germany Star Defence Medal	

No.5 lists his medals 1939/45 Star, France & Germany Star, Defence Medal

Steve's original medals; 1939-1945 Star, France & Germany Star, Defence Medal, War Medal 1939 – 1945, General Service Medal Palestine 1945 – 1948.

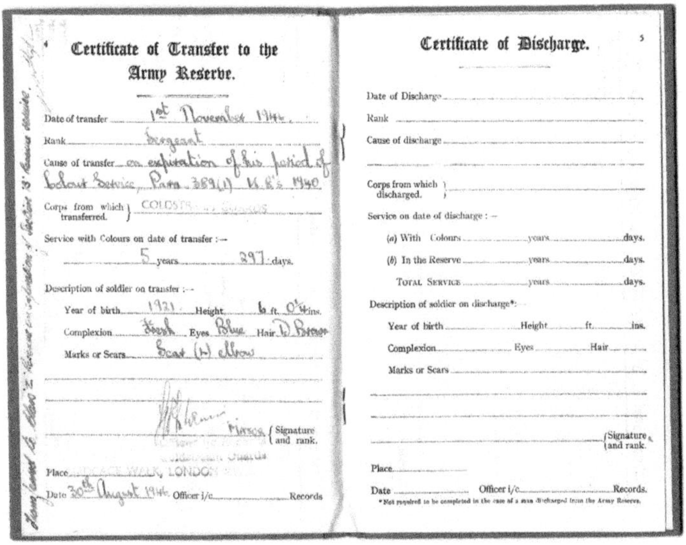

4

Certificate of Transfer to the Army Reserve.

Date of transfer 1st November 1946.

Rank Sergeant

Cause of transfer on expiration of his period of Colour Service, Para. 389(1) K.R.'s 1940

Corps from which transferred. COLDSTREAM GUARDS

Service with Colours on date of transfer :—

5 years 297 days.

Description of soldier on transfer :—

Year of birth 1921 Height 6 ft. 0¼ ins.

Complexion Fresh Eyes Blue Hair D. Brown

Marks or Scars Scar (L) elbow

Signature and rank.

Place BIRDCAGE WALK, LONDON

Date 30th August 1946 Officer i/c Records

5

Certificate of Discharge.

Date of Discharge

Rank

Cause of discharge

Corps from which discharged.

Service on date of discharge :—

(a) With Colours ... years ... days.

(b) In the Reserve ... years ... days.

Total Service ... years ... days.

Description of soldier on discharge*:

Year of birth ... Height ... ft. ... ins.

Complexion ... Eyes ... Hair ...

Marks or Scars

Signature and rank.

Place

Date ... Officer i/c ... Records.

*Not required to be completed in the case of a man discharged from the Army Reserve.

Certificate of transfer to the army reserve his date of transfer 1st November 1946, his rank Sergeant Service with colours 5 years and 297 days.

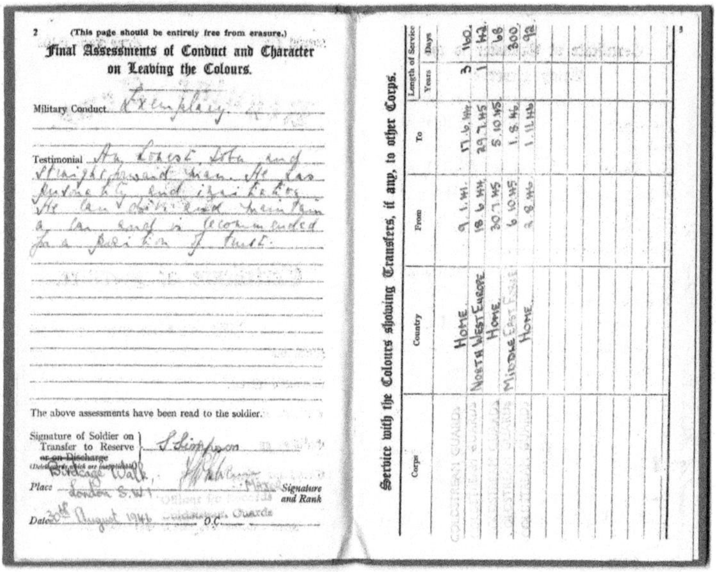

2 (This page should be entirely free from erasure.)

Final Assessments of Conduct and Character on Leaving the Colours.

Military Conduct: Exemplary

Testimonial: An honest, sober and straightforward man. He has personality and initiative. He can drive and maintain a car and is recommended for a position of trust.

The above assessments have been read to the soldier.

Signature of Soldier on Transfer to Reserve ~~or on Discharge~~ (Delete words which are inapplicable): S Simpson

Place: Birdcage Walk, London S.W.1

Signature and Rank: Officer i/c Records, Coldstream Guards

Date: 30th August 1946

Service with the Colours showing Transfers, if any, to other Corps.

Corps	Country	From	To	Length of Service Years	Length of Service Days
Coldstream Guards	Home	9.1.41	17.6.44	3	160
Coldstream Guards	North West Europe	18.6.44	29.7.45	1	42
Coldstream Guards	Home	30.7.45	5.10.45		68
Coldstream Guards	Middle East Force	6.10.45	1.8.46		300
Coldstream Guards	Home	2.8.46	1.11.46		92

In this red release book is a reference in the back for his future employers on civvy street, it reads;
Military Conduct: Exemplary
Testimonial: An honest, sober and straightforward man.
He has personality and initiative. He can drive and maintain a car and is recommended for a position of trust.
On the other page are his movements listed;
Home 9.1.41 to 17.6.44 years 3 days 160
North West Europe 18.6.44 to 29.7.45 years 1 days 42
Home 30.7.45 to 5.10.45 years 0 days 68
Middle East Force 6.10.45 to 1.8.46 years 0 days 300
Home 2.8.46 to 1.11.46 years 0 days 92

Right: A small piece of paper which has been typed. Assessment of Military Conduct 2664217 Sgt. Simpson.S. one word is typed underneath: Exemplary.

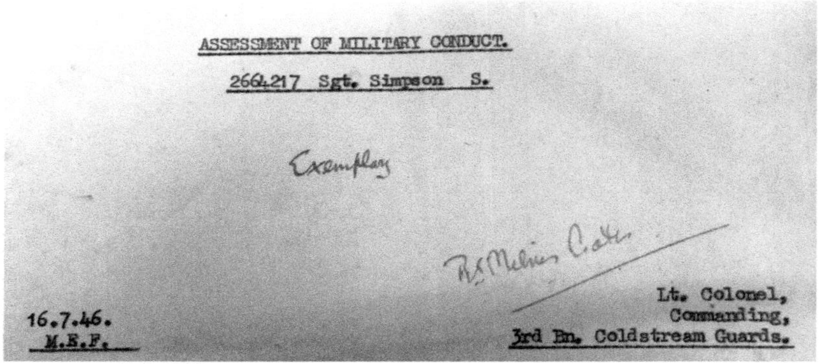

ASSESSMENT OF MILITARY CONDUCT.

2664217 Sgt. Simpson S.

Exemplary

R.S. Milnes Coates

Lt. Colonel,
Commanding,
3rd Bn. Coldstream Guards.

16.7.46.
M.E.F.

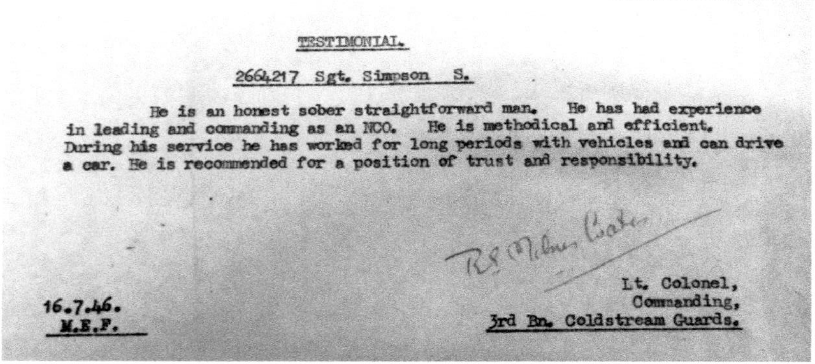

TESTIMONIAL.

2664217 Sgt. Simpson S.

He is an honest sober straightforward man. He has had experience in leading and commanding as an NCO. He is methodical and efficient. During his service he has worked for long periods with vehicles and can drive a car. He is recommended for a position of trust and responsibility.

R.S. Milnes Coates

Lt. Colonel,
Commanding,
3rd Bn. Coldstream Guards.

16.7.46.
M.E.F.

Steve's typed testimonial.

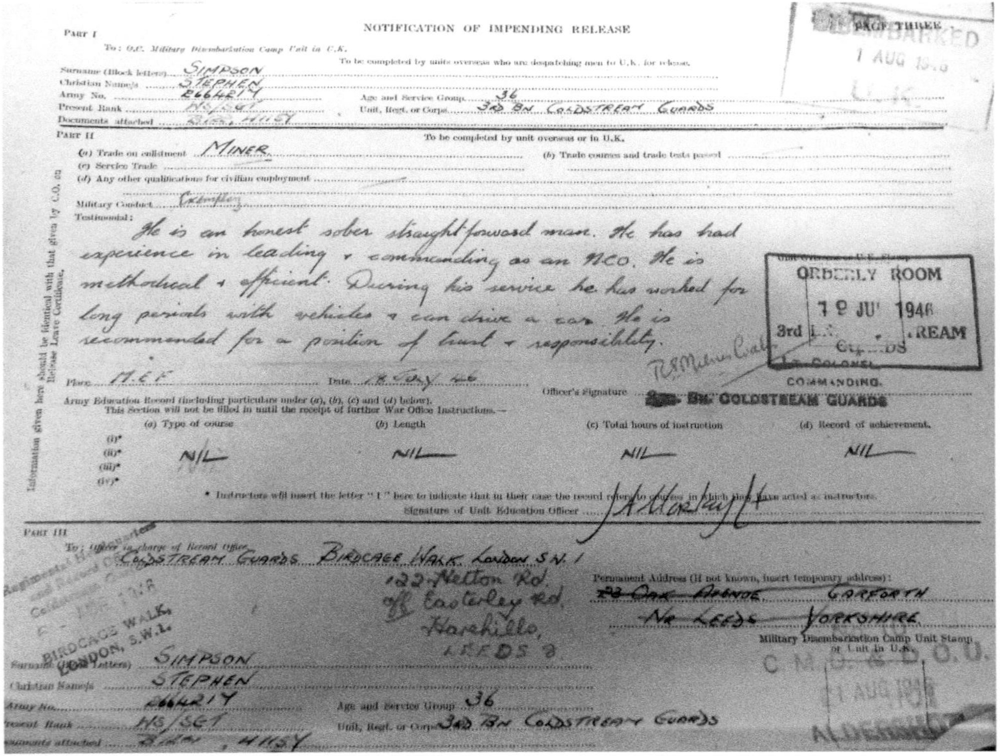
PART I

NOTIFICATION OF IMPENDING RELEASE

PAGE THREE

DISEMBARKED 1 AUG 1946 U.K.

To: O.C. Military Disembarkation Camp Unit in U.K.

To be completed by units overseas who are despatching men to U.K. for release.

Surname (Block letters) SIMPSON

Christian Name/s STEPHEN

Army No. 2664214 Age and Service Group 36

Present Rank HS/SGT Unit, Regt. or Corps 3RD BN COLDSTREAM GUARDS

Documents attached B199, H1157

PART II

To be completed by unit overseas or in U.K.

(a) Trade on enlistment MINER (b) Trade courses and trade tests passed

(c) Service Trade

(d) Any other qualifications for civilian employment

Military Conduct Exemplary

Testimonial: He is an honest sober straight forward man. He has had experience in leading + commanding as an NCO. He is methodical + efficient. During his service he has worked for long periods with vehicles + can drive a car. He is recommended for a position of trust + responsibility.

Information given here should be identical with that given by C.O. on Release Leave Certificate.

Place M.E.F. Date 18 July 46 Officer's Signature

ORDERLY ROOM 19 JUL 1946 3rd BN. COLDSTREAM GUARDS

LT. COLONEL COMMANDING 3RD BN. COLDSTREAM GUARDS

Army Education Record (including particulars under (a), (b), (c) and (d) below). This Section will not be filled in until the receipt of further War Office Instructions.—

	(a) Type of course	(b) Length	(c) Total hours of instruction	(d) Record of achievement
(i)*				
(ii)*	NIL	NIL	NIL	NIL
(iii)*				
(iv)*				

* Instructors will insert the letter "I" here to indicate that in their case the record refers to courses in which they have acted as instructors.

Signature of Unit Education Officer

PART III

To: Officer in charge of Record Office COLDSTREAM GUARDS BIRDCAGE WALK LONDON S.W.1

Regimental Headquarters and Record Office Coldstream Guards BIRDCAGE WALK, LONDON, S.W.1.

122 Netton Rd. off Easterley Rd, Harehills, LEEDS 8

Permanent Address (If not known, insert temporary address): ~~28 Oak Avenue~~ GARFORTH ~~Nr LEEDS~~ YORKSHIRE

Surname (Block Letters) SIMPSON

Christian Name/s STEPHEN

Army No. 2664214 Age and Service Group 36

Present Rank HS/SGT Unit, Regt. or Corps 3RD BN COLDSTREAM GUARDS

Documents attached B199, H1157

Military Disembarkation Camp Unit Stamp or Unit in U.K.

C.M.D. & D.O.U. 11 AUG 1946 ALDERSHOT

Another official reference of Steve's from his collection, Notification of Impending Release:

Trade on enlistment: Miner

Military Conduct: Exemplary

Testimonial: He is an honest, sober and straight forward man. He has had experiences in leading and commanding as an N.C.O. He is methodical and efficient. During his service he has worked for long periods with vehicles and can drive a car. He is recommended for a position of trust and responsibility.

This photograph has 1946 written on the back, it is notable in his face the effect of what the War did to him compared to earlier photographs taken from when he joined back in 1941.

Steve and Beryl on their wedding day 5th April 1947 at St Johns Church, Roundhay, Leeds, West Yorkshire.

Right: Steve and Beryl with their first daughter, they called her Jannine, just as he promised the little French girl he would, whom he was billeted with.

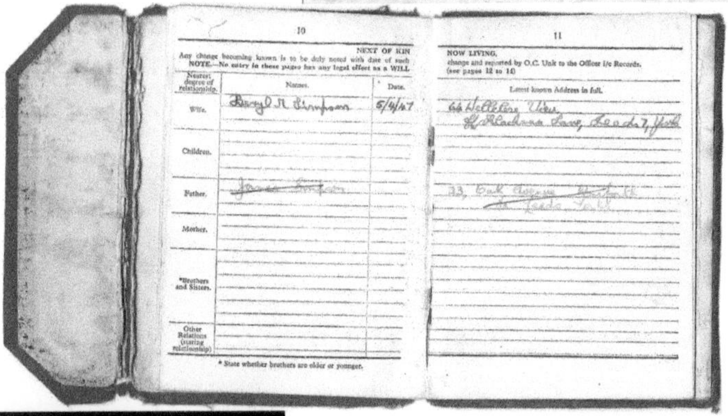

10

NEXT OF KIN

Any change becoming known is to be duly noted with date of such

NOTE.—No entry in these pages has any legal effect as a WILL.

Nearest degree of relationship.	Names.	Date.	Latest known Address in full.
Wife.	Beryl R Simpson	5/4/47	[illegible]
Children.			
Father.	~~[illegible]~~		~~[illegible]~~
Mother.			
*Brothers and Sisters.			
Other Relations (stating relationship)			

* State whether brothers are elder or younger.

11

NOW LIVING,

change and reported by O.C. Unit to the Officer i/c Records.

(see pages 12 to 14)

Above: Steve's Service Book is updated and Beryl is put in as his Wife on the 5th April 1947 their wedding day.

Left: Steve post war years.

10

'PEOPLE WOULD COME UP AND THANK US!'

'*Grandad did indeed return to Normandy for the 60th V.E. Day celebrations, this is his account.'*

Right on the 3rd June 2004 my family assembled, this included my son Stephen, my three grandsons Andrew, Charles and Richard plus my son in law Alan Morgan and my granddaughters husband David Spear. We travelled down to Portsmouth, a happy group enjoying our bottles of beer and sandwiches on the way, arriving at Portsmouth in the evening we boarded the ferry Normandy and did the overnight crossing to Ouistreham which is the Caen Port. We landed about 7.30am on June the 4th 2004 and proceeded down to Courseulles where we had arranged our billet, it's a lovely little seaside place, tidy clean holiday port. After leaving our luggage in the apartment we then went onto the cemetery at St Mauvieux where three of our friends are buried side by side, they were killed two days after landing in Normandy in June 1944, Tom Dean a Leeds Boy, Tommy Johnson he was a Leeds lad and a lad called George Cobby who I'd served with right from been recruits, we'd been together at least four years like, prior to him been killed.

'I requested a copy of the War Diary for the 28th & 29th June

1944. During our trip to the Regimental Archives it was noted that the majority of the war diary is typed, the first few days are hand written due to the ferocity of action. This is the excerpt that describes what happened to the 3 men Grandad continues to pay his respect to every time he visits Normandy, the images of the diary can be found in Fig.138'

War diary excerpt Page 44-31B Sheet VIII

1900 Carrier patrol sent out to Carpiquet aerodrome report sniper in the wood at 953675 and they were fired on from a fillhouse at 954886.

The battalion position was shelled and mortared at intervals...

War diary excerpt Page 44-31C Sheet IX

...during the day and there have been some casualties.

4 Killed 14 Wounded.

2100 Commanding officer to coordinating reinforcements at Btn HQ.'

They were killed on a patrol at the aerodrome at Carpiquet they were spotted by the Germans, they were shelled and mortared, the three of them were killed side by side and as I say, now there in the cemetery at St Mauvieux side by side. Every time we go over Jack and I, he's the fella who was in the same platoon as me, Jack Camidge, we always make a point of doing a pilgrimage and visiting their graves y'see and pay our respects.

From there we went into Caen and parked up in the main square and had a few glasses, when we'd been in Courselles early morning I'd done some shopping. We went on then to the Municipal Buildings at Caen, there was gonna be a ceremony starting at 3oclock, this area is a beautifully set out place with nice gardens in the building area itself, and parkland you can walk through. The ceremony taking place was of presenting Veterans of the Normandy Campaign with the Lapel Badge, this is a beautiful made article and its recipient had a chair marked personally, your name was on the back of the chair in alphabetical order.

The ceremony took place and the national anthems were played which was very moving, the American, French, English and Canadians, the allies anthems. Speeches were made thanking all the veterans for taking part and freeing the people of Normandy, after the speeches and so forth, I presume she was the President, a nice young lady came round to every veteran and pinned on this Veterans Badge, she thanked us like for what we'd done which was very nice, she said,

'On behalf of the people of Normandy it is their pleasure to present this badge to a Veteran.'

And thanked us for taking part in their freedom y'see, I found that the young people particularly would come up and thank us, I get emotional.

'Grandad's voice was breaking as he thought about the younger generation approaching him and thanking him for his part in the campaigns, the emotion he displayed was very humbling. He seemed taken aback by strangers been so grateful to him and his fellow comrades.'

Well I took part in The Campaigns, I was proud to have taken part, but on reflection really my immediate lot, it was easy going in when I think what had happened to the lads on D-Day itself, had to fight their way in, we landed almost dry shod, not a shot fired at us and it was only a couple of days after when we came under fire when we moved into the line you see. With us been an Armoured Division, there wasn't room at the time for the armour, so we were infantry to our tanks so they sent us over previous to the tanks, we were there two to three weeks before the armour arrived so consequently we took over part of the line. We were scheduled to do a big attack on the Carpiquet itself to take the ridge, but plans were changed fortunately, unfortunately though for the Canadians they had to do the attack over the aerodrome and they got severely mauled. There were a hell of a lot of casualties, so as I say in a way it was lucky for us and unlucky for the Canadians that had to do it, these things happen in wartime and as I say you thank your lucky stars that it wasn't you that had have to do it like.

Anyway there were children of all ages y'know from little toddlers up to adult age, it wasn't just the children, there were older people y'know, probably some that had been children at the time of the invasion, they were very grateful y'know. I found personally that the French people particularly in Normandy were very, very nice people, friendly, helpful you know, appreciative of what the allies had done to free them. I suppose it must have been awful to be oppressed by the Germans, never knowing if you were gonna be whipped off to prison camps or labour camps y'know, I suppose that was one of the reasons why they were so grateful. I don't suppose the poor people that had their houses and farms and what not battered, felt so appreciative at the time. The destruction in parts of Normandy was absolutely horrific particularly Caen, which was bombed and shelled bombed and shelled you know.

Saw one raid myself there, one thousand bombers went in one night and it was awful to watch y'know, we were outside Caen and we saw the bombers come in and like I say it was terrific the barrage that went up against them, some of the planes were hit, I saw one go down in flames, funnily enough later on, when we did a big attack a thousand bombers preceded our advance and I saw a plane shot down again.

Now then, while I've been over this last time, this was on the 17th July 2004 my last visit, our division had a ceremony at a place called Cagny and that was as far as we got in our three Armoured Divisions attack, we were absolutely mauled but we managed to get to Cagny on the 18th July.

- Brussels Sprout No.4 18th – 19th July 1944:
  Took part in Operation GOODWOOD to enlarge the bridge

head in front of the newly captuyred CAEN. Battalion took over position in area of CAINY from Armed Bde.

Brussels Sprout Diary

On the 17th July 2004 was the actual day the Guards Armoured Division had a ceremony in Cagny to commemorate the event like, they visited the cemetery where the boys were buried. There was also a big military display in another area of the old wartime vehicles, following that we went to a civilian cemetery, it was just a small ceremony and it was a crew of a Bomber's that had been shot down in this particular raid so they had a ceremony there too, the French civilians had buried the crew in their cemetery, so they were left there like, not moved to a military cemetery. As I say, it was a very moving little ceremony that took part there, but you'd mixed feelings y'know going round the different areas, after the ceremony, we were presented with our Veterans Lapel Badge.

We decided then, well me been leader of the pack, decided that I would go and show the family with me, Pegasus Bridge, it was very good we also visited the Paratrooper's Museum, The Pegasus Bridge is obviously history now. The Paratroopers on the dawn of D-Day 6th June, they came in, soldiers captured the bridge and it was a brilliant piece of arms y'know, consequently they named the bridge Pegasus after the Paratroopers y'see, so it was a nice session there at Pegasus Bridge on June 4th 2004. So on the 18th July 2004 I was back at Pegasus Bridge which I'd crossed sixty years earlier to go into my first action with my Division, in the Paratroopers area which is on the far side of the river they have their museum and the original bridge that the paratroopers had captured. It's in their museum area so considering it was sixty years previously that I had gone over that bridge, I decided sixty years after almost to the day, well it was on the exact date and almost to the hour, I walked back over that bridge just for old times sake y'see, never thinking sixty years ago that I'd be fit and able to do it.

Moving on from that I visited Normandy again with three of my old army pals, Sprout Beasley who served in Italy and North Africa, Billy Bristow who served in the 5th Battalion in Normandy, I didn't know Bill at the time its only since coming out and been a civilian that we got acquainted, and Jack Walker who was a younger solider so he had no warfare dealing but he was very, very interested in what had happened y'see.

The family party back in the June were very interested in all that was happening and on the Saturday June 5th I said I'd take them into Arromanches, to show them where the troops had fought ashore.

It was a nice beautiful afternoon in Arromanches, then I said,

'Right 'o' the next port is the Omaha Cemetery where 9000 American Service people are buried.'

It was a beautiful sunny day, I let the boys wander around and I took a few photographs and they were photographing, they also went over the headland looking out on to the beach where the Americans had come ashore and faced all the slaughtering y'know. It was absolutely mad the way they had to come ashore, it wasn't particularly high cliffs, y'know but the Germans were dug in on top and they had machine guns and they were spraying all the beach like, how anybody got ashore and got up amongst the Germans is amazing y'know. While we were there, there were French and American boys, Soldiers each with their countries flag, they were stood side by side like, a French man then American, Frenchman then American and so on, they were rehearsing for the ceremony for when the president was arriving on D-Day, which was the Sunday. It was quite a ceremony y'know with bagpipes and everything, everything was on television too, so a lot probably saw all that was happening.

Evening time we moved back into Coursellles and had a nice 'scough up' and a few drinks, then coming to Sunday which was D-Day we decided that we wouldn't go into Arromanches for the ceremony because it was absolutely chock a block with old soldiers and families like, so we decided that we'd spend the day in Courselles and on the plaza was a massive TV screen so we didn't miss anything that was happening. Now then it turned out we couldn't get out of Courselles if we had wanted, because with all the Presidents y'know, and the Queen in the area, the French President, the Russian President the German President they were all in the area moving around, so the Armed Guards were covering all the streets and the roads. It was almost impossible to get out from where we were staying, it turned out to be absolutely heaving y'know, it was amazing, Jack and I were particularly amazed, there were people of all ages, all nationalities, they all wanted to talk to us y'know.

'At this point Grandad started to get upset again, there was a long pause.'

I don't know what's up with me, I suppose it hadn't been until then you'd think about what you had done, as I say there were people of all ages all nationalities came to Jack Camidge and I we were together sat on a wall. And they were young and old, all blooming nationalities, they wanted to speak to us it was a bit moving y'know when a child would come up and say,

'Thank you'

'Grandad was crying as he was speaking now, he paused again for some composure, it was really humbling listening to him talk about this moving experience, the dawning of the reality of his words breaking through.'

There was one incident where a young lady with her mother came up and wanted to take a photograph with an old veteran, we said certainly. She was visiting from Paris with her mother so we obliged the young lady and in appreciation she gave me a little souvenir from Paris which was a little key chain, with the Eiffel tower hung on. Like I say people come up and were just curious as to what sort of life we'd lived y'know, how we'd coped y'know, one chap said,

'Now then after 60 years what's your feeling against the Germans?'

'Grandad started to get upset again.'

'Well' I said 'I've no particular feeling, apart from the vicious lot like the SS Gestapo. The ordinary German Soldier was like us, he was told what he'd got to do like we had, I have no animosity to him now like.' I says.

When I took them prisoner I said, it had gone then, he was out of it I had no harsh feelings towards him, I don't know whether I were one alone, I think everybody had the same feeling regarding it y'see. Anyway that was one thing I was asked and I'd never given it thought previously really until that person asked me, it wasn't that they were been funny it was just that they had a genuine interest too.

Then three smart young lads come walking up, well I'm saying young lads they were probably in there forties or fifties and we had a bit of joking, you could tell with their stance they were Guardsman like y'see, one were a Scotch Guard and he said,

'I was in the Scotch Guards such and such a Battalion, my friend here, now I know what your gonna say, he was in the Grenadiers.'

'Well we'll talk to ya like' I says.

There's always that rivalry, particularly between the Grenadiers and the Coldstreamers' you see, so I said

'Well it doesn't matter if you are in the Grenadiers, well talk to you like seen as its D-Day we'll talk to you.' And we had a bit of banter with them like and off they went, and even they thanked us.

'Grandad started to get choked up again with emotion'

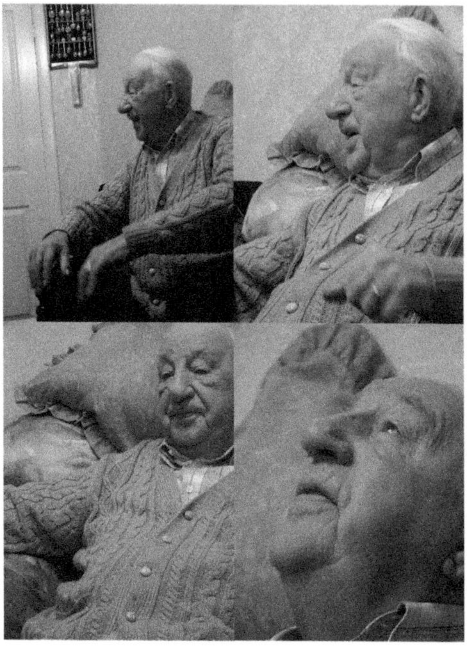

When we were just chatting they were asking what it was like to be under fire and that sort of thing y'know, how did you get home? What were your feelings, your thoughts at the time? That sort of thing, well we told 'em we were shit scared and it wasn't nice been shelled and mortared with bullets whistling round ya, but you had good friends and you could laugh at things afterwards like, which had frightened you at the time y'see.

Basically it was all the same questions; What we felt like going into action? How did we live? How we were fed? And that sort of thing.

I was describing more to Andrew my grandson and there was a young lady listening, apparently in this recent conflict the gulf, the troops were sent haphazard, without proper ammunitions and armour and so on, in our particular war everything was catered for even down to sick bags when you were crossing the channel. We were issued with a 24 hour pack, each man was drawn French Francs, y'know liberation money they called it, every conceivable thing you think of had been organised you see, so when we landed with a 24 hour ration pack which was condensed stuff like, dehydrated and all that sort of stuff, then you had an emergency, it was in a tin, it was a chocolate, concentrated chocolate food thing, that was never to be used unless ordered by an officer y'know. If there was no food at all, say you were in a position where you couldn't be fed, Officers would say,

'Right you use that chocolate.'

It really was a state of emergency thing, then the food they had, what they call a 14 man ration box pack was food for the whole day for fourteen men. There was four varieties or was it five varieties of different food in them so you wouldn't get the same one every day so you'd have a change of food like. In this ration box they'd be 5 cigarettes per man, 3 solid fruit lollies, hard-boiled sweets a bar of chocolate, which was special chocolate, 3 pieces of toilet paper, and say a particular box for breakfast might be tinned bacon. There was a tin with biscuits, hard tack biscuits really tough biscuits you wanted a real crunch for them. Then for lunch it might be a steak and kidney pudding and for a sweet it might be rice pudding or a rich fruit pudding, all tinned, which had to be heated up. For tea meal it might be salmon, a tin of salmon or sardines or something like that, then for a supper to make a supper meal there was a concentrated very thick soup, all enough for fourteen men, it all had to be heated and cooked up y'see. So the tins they had their use, what we used to do with the biscuit tin which was about 10 inches square and probably about 5 inches deep, we use to cut the lid of, fill it with soil pour petrol in and you'd drop a match in and that was your cooker, then another biscuit tin you'd probably use for a heater for your water, the water, ooh it was foul tasting, it was chlorinated water y'see. The tea itself was a mixture of sugar, milk and tea and you'd to stir it, when the water was on the boil you'd add the tea stirring all the time, the first few cups were manky, but you gradually got used to the taste of it and it was eventually like nectar y'know, particularly when you'd been under shellfire and your nerves were jangling. The old five cigarettes used to get some stick then and the old teapot like y'know.

Then the box itself if you were in a static position, a pit would be dug and the box would go over the pit with a hole cut in it and a lid on it and that was used as a latrine y'see so everything had a use. For three months we were on this particular type of ration and eventually we started getting white bread which was really, really something y'see, as the bakeries had started to come over then. Then we started been issued with soft rations, which was flour and all that sort of thing, and we use to do our own cooking like, we were fed quite well really. We were very fortunate if you compare our soldiering to what the lads in Italy and Africa had to go through and the poor fellas in Burma. What an existence they must have had, it was awful and evil was our war but comparing it to say Burma I'm pleased I took part in Normandy as opposed to going out there. Anyway that's how we used to live y'see and we'd take it turns and anyone who was handy at cooking and anything we could scrounge potatoes or anything like that we'd make use of.

So going back to this young lady who was listening as I talked to Andrew, she was all ears y'know like, I suppose it must have been a revelation to her y'know, how we survived.

Then going back to the day in Courseulles this young boy probably 12 or 13 years old came up with his little book and he wanted our signatures in it y'know and what Regiment and where we'd been and he came back later, he wanted to have a photograph taken, with us.

'Grandad's voice was breaking again with emotion.'

So we obliged him and off he went chuffed to little apples

y'know. So as I say we had a very lovely day in Courseulles and my thoughts now of course, 60 years on, its amazing how the country has recovered y'know the places have been rebuilt and I must say the cleanliness of the place, be it a village, it's absolutely spotless its really a credit to the people who live there, when I come and see the sate of our cities and the streets I'm disgusted you know.

So all in all the trip I was pleased with that and me family had seen that we'd done our bit for the country.

The boys were very respectful of all that had taken part, particularly when we went to the cemeteries I think it must have shook them when they realised how many lads and the ages of some of them y'know that's what got 'em talking, I say 18 years old 19 y'know. As I say I'm glad I'd taken part in the preceding and I was sorry about the people that had lost their lives y'know, young men that should have been enjoying life, just obliterated it was sad. One thing that used to get me if I went round the cemeteries if it was written on the headstone, 'Unknown British Solider' y'know, that use to get me, I think some poor person must think, I wonder if that's my son.

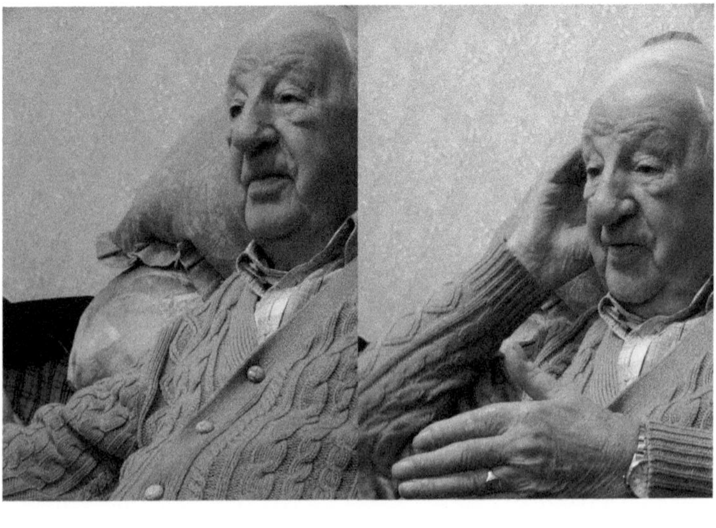

'Grandad broke down and started crying. He took a moment to recover.'

So by enlarge my trip to Normandy with my family was a success, stepping back in time to memories made me thankful that I'd got through ok and give thanks that somebody was looking after me and I got through, sound in wind and limb. As I say it was nice to go with my son and grandsons, sixty years ago I never visualised anything like that happening, although funnily enough I thought nothing could happen to me. It was a silly thought but my mother died when I was young and I always had the thought that she was up there y'know, looking after me and I know it sounds daft that, but I suppose that's what you think, in my case I think it was thinking like that, that kept my mind and I didn't go bomb hoppy or anything like that y'see. You used to wonder at times if you were gonna get through y'know, particularly if you were going into an attack and you didn't know what you were going to meet up with, then when the attack was over you'd probably start digging in. The Germans kept raining on you and mortaring and shelling you and you couldn't get down deep enough in them days y'know, but that's the way it went and as I say I give thanks every day that I got through ok and I feel sorry for the lads that didn't get through you know. In some way or another it doesn't leave you y'know and it doesn't matter what Regiment you were, when you were in action like that in your own family regiment you could appreciate the other lads y'know whatever Regiment or Court they were in you were all in it together.

It's made me appreciate life, its made me give thanks that I've led a pretty healthy life and active life when I think of some of the atrocious things that happened to some fellas and the wounds that they received y'know, I give thanks every day. It were difficult coming out of the army to settle down, in fact I almost went back into the army you know, in the early days just after I'd come out I missed the companionship of comrades real comrades y'know. The friendships that were formed particularly with the lads who I'd served with for a number of years we'd lived and slept together, got drunk together and those thing young lads do y'know, you have a kinship; in fact you could say a brother-ship really with that type of fella, in fact with any service man that had been in campaigns, you have an affinity sort of thing you know. Funnily enough I was sat on a bench yesterday in the Arndale Shopping Centre, I was waiting for some films to be developed and this old gentlemen come and sat aside of me and we started talking, it turned out he'd been in the REME as I recall the REME was formed at the end of 1941 they took chaps from the RASC and the Ordnance and they were the Royal Electrical and Mechanical Engineers. I told him one of our fellas had to serve in the orderly room when the Battalion was formed and he volunteered for the REME, he came back to us later as our Platoon Fitter, it turned out I mentioned he'd been at Scarborough,

'Oh' he said 'I'd been at Scarborough.' I says

'Oh were you at Guards Armoured Division?'

'Aye' he says 'that's right we were tanks, were you a Guardsman?' I said

'Yes I was 5th Battalion, we were infantry to tanks.'

'Aye we were Light Aids Department for one of the units like y'know say L.A.D.'

So as I say we'd a lot in common to say we were complete strangers we'd a sort of a kinship there y'see, so that's the one result of us serving like in those days y'know as a wartime solider. That's just one incident, I mean wherever you go there's always somebody, you've got a friend somewhere whichever part of the country you go to, you start talking to somebody of your age group and 'Oh yes I was so and so, oh yes I were there like!' So its, well I suppose it's a worldwide comradeship y'know, I mean like with Canadians, I was talking to some Canadian lads and they served along side of us, in fact it was a Canadian unit that had gone through us at this attack at Carpiquet y'know. It's amazing how once you start talking how things come together y'know.

Civilian life it took getting use to after six years of wartime soldiering like, but I'd met your Nana during the war and we got married after I came out, a year after I came out.

'Grandad married my Nana, Beryl May Clough on April 5th 1947 at St Johns Church, Roundhay, Leeds.'

I did miss the life; even at my age now I still have longings for it you know, I wish I was a young man again, although saying that I don't think I'd be an Infantryman if I ever went in again you were up at the front as an Infantry Man like, although all the other lads they clobbered whatever their jobs were, but it seemed to be short measured for the Infantry Man y'know he was at the spear edge sort of thing. Even today, it's still the Infantry Man that's got the job to do at the start of the thing.

By enlarge I have a great respect for our soldiers, when I came home I kept in touch with some of the lads, my comrades. Over the years regrettably they keep dwindling on me and my circle of correspondence has declined y'know, I'd a friend who was in my Platoon he was a Sergeant Percy Kent, lovely fella he lived down in Essex and every year we'd corresponded we never missed a year and then on the odd occasion when we'd go to Memorial Weekend I'd meet him in London like for an hour or two it was lovely, sadly Percy died. I had another friend he were a, he'd won a Military Medal a fella called Pete Jordan he lived down in Kent, he kept in touch and I'd see him occasionally at Memorial Weekend, he'd informed me he'd got heart trouble and he had a rough path. A few years back I decide I would go down one weekend and see him like y'see and it upset me when I did see him like, I remembered a big strapping fella and he were an ex-policemen and to see him there suffering from Parkinson Disease and he'd got his problems. I did take him out the Sunday morning, regrettably the September he up't and died.

Then over the years the ranks have depleted and I'm sad to say there's very few of us in the Leeds area that served together, they have gone now like, I think I can only think of Jack Camidge, I see him regularly and meet up with him. I have a friend out on the Platoon in Hull Eric Lord and another old buddy of mine we were recruits together and we served all the time together until Bill was wounded and he lives in Tong Bradford, I see him on the odd occasion, Bill Wigglesworth. So as I say there about the only ones I have contact with now.

Steve at home in a Bren Gun Carrier during
a visit to Normandy 1994.

Excerpt from the original Battalion War Diary
from the archives at RHQ.

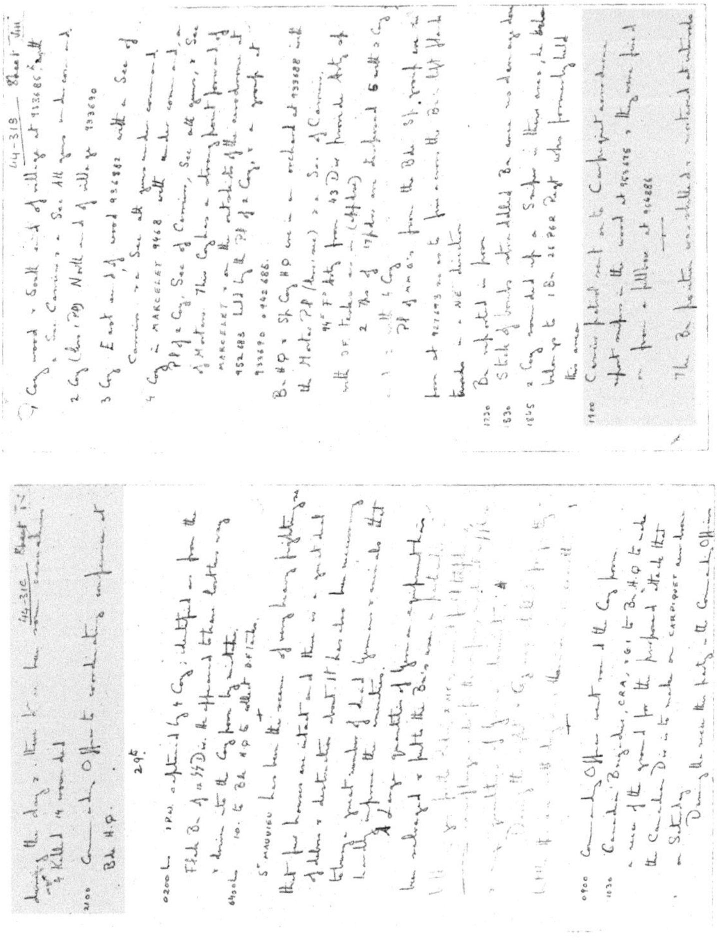

60th D Day celebrations Arromanches Beach when the veterans marched passed Royalty.

Jack Camidge and Steve in centre as they were part of the veterans marching on Arromanches.

Steve on left and Jack Camidge on right signing a remembrance / visitors book.

Steve's commemorative WWII VE VJ Veterans badge.

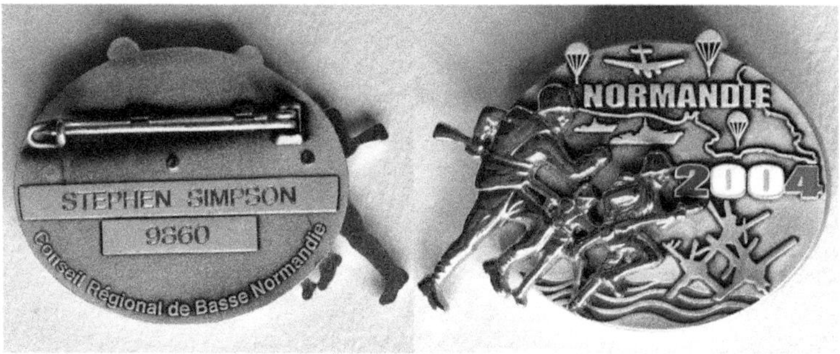

Vetrans Badge presented to Steve during 60th D Day celebrations in Normandy, worn in the photograph of Steve at the Municipal Buildings, Caen on page 180.

Allie lapel badge also worn by Steve in the photograph of him at the Municipal Buildings, Caen.

Steve resting in the shade after been presented with his Veterans' Lapel Badge at the Municipal Buildings, Caen.

Steve on left and Jack Camidge right, I love the accidental yet fitting sign on the shop window behind them in this shot.

Steve's Beret and medals as worn in the photograph on page 180.

Normandy 2004:
Charles Simpson (Grandson)
Jack Camidge Richard Simpson (Grandson)
Andrew Simpson (Grandson)
Stephen Simpson (Son)
Steve himself.

11

'THE COLDSTREAM GUARDS ASSOCIATION'

The Coldstream Guards Association is for old Coldstreamer's to get together periodically and chat of old times and organise a bit of a social life and so on. The Leeds branch was formed in 1946 well I was demobbed in 1946 and I joined the branch when I came out and I've been a member ever since, so you could say I'm a founder member of the Leeds branch. Although that's the Coldstream Guards Association as such, it was called 'Old Coldstreamer's' the first time round and they were formed probably about 1914 or something like that, gradually they spread around the country all through the country right up to the Scottish Borders y'see, it's an old boys squad like y'know and its nice to meet up with lads that served through war and chaps throughout the years that have served and they get together, they do say that were a family that the guards The Coldstream Family they call it, once a Coldstreamer always a Coldstreamer, it's true, like I say I could go to china and I'd see the fella with the Brigade Tie on and I'll say,

'Now then what unit were you in?'

'The Coldstream.'

And you've a friend especially if he's a Coldstreamer particularly y'know. So unfortunately, well I don't know, I don't think other regiments have the same sort of get together the Guards do, they do have gatherings but not to the extent the Regalia Guard's do y'know. They have a memorial Guards Parade, there's the Guards Memorial there, it's the five regiments Grenadiers, Coldstream, Scots, Irish and Welsh Guards and every year each regiment has a memorial weekend and all the lads gather in London and they march from the barracks with the band down to Horse Guard Parade. There's a short service and they lay a wreath, ours takes part every May, sometimes the Chapel is over-flowing and as I say you fall in, in your old battalions or your war time battalion, because the ranks have depleted every year you join the 4th & 5th Battalions they were war time battalions. You walk down Birdcage Walk out of Wellington Barracks onto Horse Guards Parade and then there's a short service, then the Colonel of the Regiment lays the wreath and you march back with the band, you see old men of 70, as soon as the band starts they grow a foot, it's amazing what a difference that makes hearing that band on a Regimental March. They come from all over the country and world visiting from Canada, Australia, New Zealand, arranging trips around that time so they can take part.

A small plaque amongst Grandad's artefacts from the Coldstream Guards Association.

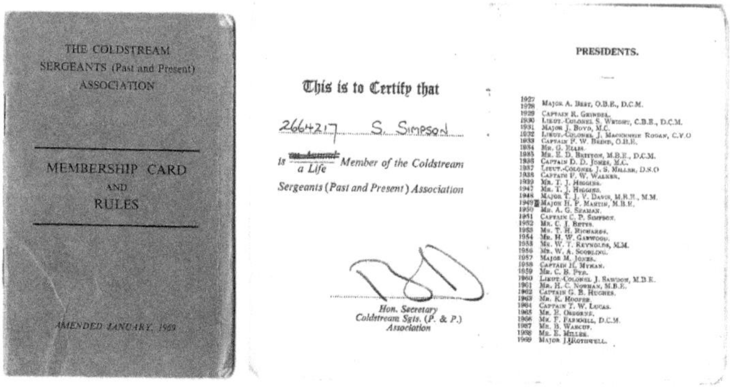

1969 Membership card with rules for the association.

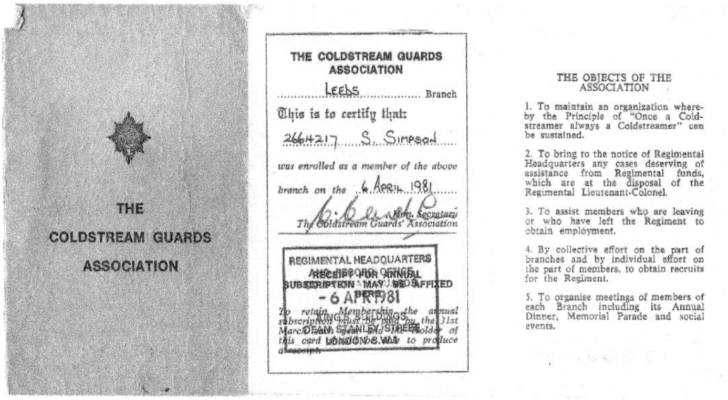

Membership card with rules for the association 1981

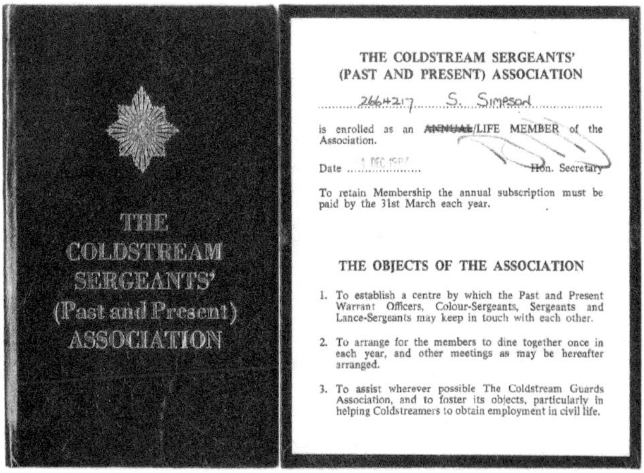

Membership card with rules for the association 1984

Membership cards of the Sergeants (Past & Present) Association, Coldstream Guards Association, War Office 1946 issued Regimental and Old Comrades Associations Rules and Customs of the Guards Book.

12

'NO ONE SAID A WORD'

'Grandad attended many Coldstream Guards dinners both locally and across the country with other branches as well as down in London he kept every menu and ticket, he even kept the very first Menu from 1945 that his comrades signed whilst they were still in Europe. This is a short story told by Steve's son about one of those dinners.'

It was around 1984 the Coldstream Guards Association, Doncaster Branch were holding an annual dinner, my Dad and I were going along to a venue in Doncaster one evening and I went to Crossgates to pick him up from his house, he got in the car and was carrying a spare Coldstream Colours dress tie and a suit jacket. I didn't really question it at the time even though he was wearing them already with his suit He told me to call over at Castleford, as we were going to give his mate a lift to the dinner, he was also a Coldstream Guard WWII veteran, my Dad had paid for his friends dinner ticket as a kind gesture. We proceeded to a small house in Castleford, Dad's friend was so happy to see him and was so grateful when he realised my Dad had brought him a spare regimental tie to wear to the dinner.

We went into his house, it didn't have much inside at all, and hardly any furniture or comforts I could tell that he was very poor. He stood in his old trousers and pyjama jacket top and put the tie on, I thought he was going to get changed and put on something else, but he didn't have anything else to wear, he couldn't afford it so we left and got in the car as he was. We all drove to the dinner at Doncaster and walked into the venue, it was lovely and everyone was dressed formally, Dad's friend came in with us wearing his pyjama top and old trousers, I didn't know what to expect when we walked in and people in the room looked over to us.

Immediately the veterans and guardsmen at the dinner all came over to say hello and not one person batted an eyelid at the man in his pyjama top, they treated Dad's friend, a fellow Coldstreamer with as much respect as they did me and my Dad. All evening this man sat in his pyjamas wearing his Coldstream tie with such pride, he conversed with his old comrades and younger Coldstream Guards, we sat through dinner and had a lovely time, I was simply humbled that absolutely no one mentioned his pyjama's or gave him a funny look, he was treated with the respect and honour he deserved for been a Coldstream Guard Veteran, one who had served King and country.

'A persons true character is shown when they carry out acts that no one else may ever see or know about, this story is so moving and encapsulates how Steve valued his comrades, and how they value each other. It is important that we understand and respect what our forces have done for our freedom today, and continue to do, it helps us to understand why Steve kept all these things and marked his journey as if it is one of the most important stories to be told, because it is.

Over the years we may forget words, what people have told us or said to us, but we never forget how someone makes us feel, Grandad seemed to have the power to put a smile on anyone's face and make them feel warm, respected and loved, what a gift.'

The first Menu from 1945 and thereafter official original Coldstream Guards Dinners menus 1945 to 1959

Coldstream Guards Association original menus through the 60's and 70's.

Coldstream Guards Association Dinner menus through the 80's up to 2006.

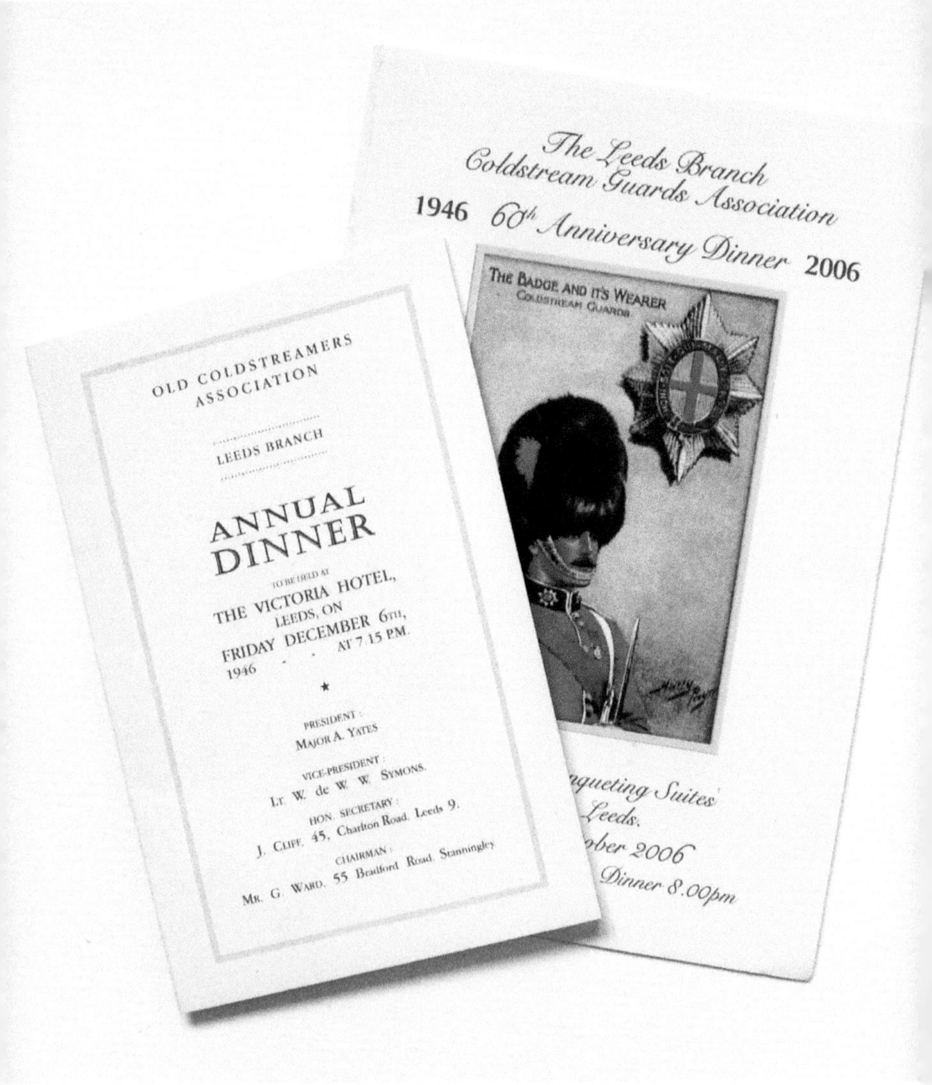

The 1946 original menu was copied for the 2006 Coldstream Guards 60th Anniversary Dinner with a note inside reading; 'A copy of the original menu has been reproduced thanks to Steve Simpson.'

Steve's
Coldstream
Guards
Cravat.

Steve's Coldstream Guards Tie.

Steve's
smaller
medals used
for dress.

13

'BE PROUD TO BE A BRITAIN'

I loved it, I loved that regiment, I've been a member of the association since 1946 I was one of the early birds, I've seen some comings and goings, I'm proud of that bloody regiment I'm proud of the lads who serve it, the Coldstream Guards Regiment to date have more operational tours than any other in the army, the Coldstream Guards do get pushed wherever there's a scrap and it were the same in my day, with the old 5th battalion, where the shit were flying we were shoved in, and more often than not the mission was accomplished, that may be part of the reason why they feel the Coldstream Guards are capable of doing things.

'When asked to give a final message here was my Grandad's response.'

'Be proud to be a Britain to start with, be proud of our military and take pride in what our youth military has done for this country over the last 100 years. Have respect for the people who gave their lives because there were a hell of a lot, well I say they gave it, but it was taken from them their lives, it was taken.

If there were a message to give the younger lads now in the regiment it would be; Be proud that you're a Guards Man, you're following in the footsteps of some great fellas and if you can equal their capability you'll be top man. There are some great fellas and we lost some an all. That would be my message to you all.'

Right: Steve during the interview.

Left: A modern Coldstream Guards Pin Badge.

Right: Steve's modern Coldstream Guard Pin Badge with Bear Skin Hat.

Left: Another Coldstream Guards Regimental Button from Steve's collection.

14

'TIRELESS WORKER'

'*My Grandad passed away aged 85 in April 5th 2009 on his wedding anniversary and has been sorely missed every day by everyone in the family. When he died the Yorkshire Evening Post ran a lovely article about him (see facing page).*'

Here is a quote from the article by Bruce Smith;

When Leeds-born Mr Simpson volunteered in 1940 as a 17-year-old, he gave the recruiting sergeant a form showing he was born two years earlier than his actual 1923 birth date. He was posted to the newly-formed 5th Battalion of the Guards Armoured Division. He spent years training as a Bren Gun Carrier Driver across the UK in readiness for the launch of the Second Front to liberate Europe from Nazi shackles.

It was while in Palestine that he experienced one of his proudest moments when he was charged with driving Field Marshall Bernard Montgomery when he visited troops in the Holy Land. He earned numerous campaign medals including the Normandy Landings and France and German Defence medals.

After his de-mob in 1946, he married his wife Beryl and helped launch the Leeds Coldstream's Guards Association.

He joined Lloyds Bank as a bank messenger and later worked for many years driving its armoured bullion delivery vehicles.'

At the end of this chapter are photographs of the remaining artefacts from Steve's collection which included the beautiful famous poem 'Just A Common Soldier' by A. Lawrence Vaincourt.

Tireless worker for ex-army comrades dies, 85

ARMY SERVICE: Sgt Steve Simpson in Palestine; and, *left*, at Nomandy with another Coldstream guardsman Jack Camidge

BY BRUCE SMITH

A MAN who lied about his age to join the army early in the Second World War and later became a tireless worker for his old comrades has died.

Sgt Steve Simpson, who landed in France a week after the Normandy Landings, was always grateful he returned from the fighting without a scratch.

So after his demob he became a founder member of the Leeds Coldstream Guards Association in 1946. He held all its senior positions and dedicated himself to helping fellow former guardsmen for over 60 years.

When Leeds-born Mr Simpson volunteered in 1940 as a 17-year-old, he gave the recruiting sergeant a form showing he was born two years earlier than his actual 1923 birth date.

He was posted to the newly-formed 5th Battalion of the Guards Armoured Division. He spent years training as a Bren Gun Carrier Driver across the UK in readiness for the launch of the Second Front to liberate Europe from Nazi shackles.

He palled-up with another Guardsman Jack Camidge, who was to become a life-long friend.

After the landings he fought all the way across France and into Germany including crossing the Rhine. In August 1944 he and Jack were parted when Jack suffered a shrapnel wound, but Steve was able to continue fighting up to the German surrender in May 1945.

Later that year after his Battalion was disbanded and an extended leave in Britain, he and his comrades were transferred to 3rd Battalion and shipped out to Palestine for a peace-keeping role.

It was while in Palestine that he experienced one of his proudest moments when he was charged with driving Field Marshall Bernard Montgomery when he visited troops in the Holy Land. He earned numerous campaign medals including the Normandy Landings and France and German Defence medals.

After his demob in 1946, he married his wife Beryl and helped launch the Leeds Coldstreams Guards Association.

He joined Lloyds Bank as a bank messenger and later worked for many years driving its armoured bullion delivery vehicles.

Mr Simpson, who died in St James's Hospital, Leeds, aged 85, on Sunday April 5, is survived by his wife, their four children, Janine, 61, twins Christine and Stephen, 56, and Gillian, 44, grandchildren and seven great grandchildren.

Outside his family his work for the Leeds Coldstream Association was his main interest.

Mr Camidge said: "Steve was a popular sergeant in the army and he was a great worker for our association."

bruce.a.smith@ypn.co.uk

A copy of the original article which his Grandson Charles framed.

Courtesy of the Yorkshire Evening Post

By Bruce Smith 13th April 2009

This is a Guards Regimental Sergeant Major cloth badge reading Dieu Et Mon Droit meaning God and my right. It's the motto of the Monarch UK.

This is a cloth badge representing the 56th London Infantry Division, we are unsure where he got this badge from as he was not in this division.

This is a Royal Artillery Tunic Button, it was amongst Steve's collection and found in an old Thornton's Toffee Tin.

This is an old pendant which has the Italian word on it 'Primo' translated meaning prize, the image of a rifle target shoot.

A WWI medal found amongst Steve's collection of war memorabilia, we are uncertain of the provenance of this particular item. Called the Fire Cross and is awarded by the kingdom of Belgium, this is a military combat service medal eligible to Belgium Citizens and Foreign Nationals. Awarded for WWI service in the Belgium Armed Forces.

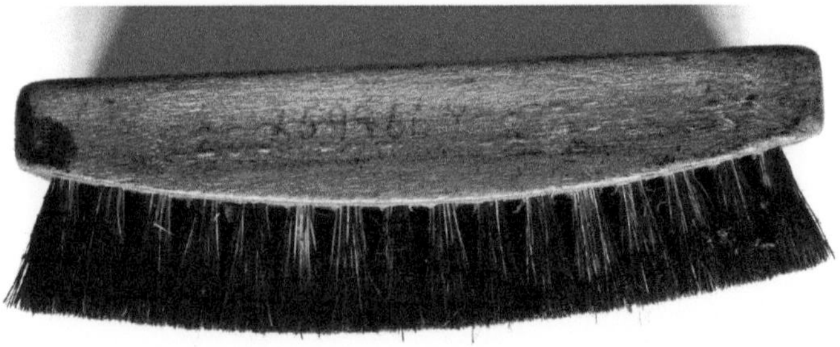

An old Army shoe brush with a role number on, 2599667.
Steve's own number was 2664217 it is uncertain who's
this is and why Steve had it.

This is a small box and contains the stripes of an unknown soldier and
is addressed to a home in Walton, we are unsure why Steve had this.

Steve's collection of commemorative booklets and certificates. He attended many remembrance services and dinners out of respect.

Steve, Remembrance Sunday Leeds circa 2006

15

'THE BRUSSEL SPROUT'

'This is the full copy of The Brussel Sprout document from Grandad's collection, which is a replica of the original battalion war diary which can be found in the archives at Wellington Barracks, the Coldstream Guards Head Quarters.'

THE BRUSSELS SPROUT

No.33 **Friday 11th 1945**

THE BATTALIONS LAST ACTION.

On the 4th May No 4 company crossed the river Oste and entered the village of HECHTHAUSEN without opposition – though a gunner tank was blown up on a sea mine, and the enemy had attempted unsuccessfully to blow up the bridge with depth charges, and this was the battalions last act of war.

Early the next morning the following message was received:-

"Germans surrendered unconditionally at 1820 hours 4th May. Hostilities on all sectors Army front will cease at 0800hours today. No repeat, No advances beyond present frontlines without orders from H.Q."

And having brought events up to the end of the war in Europe "The Brussels Sprout" is now left with nothing to do but say goodbye, and offer as a final feature the attached summary of the war diary of all the major moves and battles since the battalion arrived in NORMANDY.

8th ARMY LINK UP WITH THE RUSSIANS.

Red Army troops in Czechoslovakia are attacking the German troops still ignoring the general surrender. German lanes again attacked a concentration camp. British 8th Army troops have linked up with the Russians in AUSTRIA

West of GRAZ. The BENES returned to PRAGUE yesterday. The notorious Sudeten leader HENLIEN surrendered to the Americans.

CHANNEL ISLANDS FREED.

The CHANNEL ISLANDS were freed early on Wednesday morning when a small party of British troops landed on GUERNSEY after the Germans had signed unconditional terms aboard the British destroyed "Bulldog". As our men went ashore every building flew the union jack and there was scenes of tremendous enthusiasm.

GERMAN FLEET SURRENDERING.

The Germans in DENMARK expect to get most of their troops out within four weeks. Most of what is left of The German fleet has surrendered to the Royal Navy in COPENHAGEN Harbour. Five U Boats surrendered in British waters yesterday. Six more have been spotted flying the surrender flags.

BATTALION CASUALITIES.

Since the last issue the following casualties have been suffered by the Bn.

Wounded.
2667806 Gdsm Brown J.(4:
2667870 Gdsm Pearce P.(4: (Now re-joined unit:.
2653973 L/Cpl Hunt H. (Sp:Died of wounds.

The u/m "Died of wounds" and were not "killed in action" as stated in the last issue:-

2662985 L/Cpl Clough G. (1:
2666750 Gdsm Wilkins B.(2:
2658387 Gdsm Hunter R. (4:
2667271 Gdsm Robinson G.(3:

Summary from battalion war diary - Normandy to Victory.

1944

1. 23 June Arrived in NORMANDY. Concentration area S.W of BAYEUX.

2. 26 June-11 July: Took over defensive position at ST MAUVIEUX prior to and during the Canadian attack on CAEN.

3. 11 July-17 July: Back in rest area of BAYEUX.

4. 18 July-19 July: Took part in operation "GOODWOOD" to enlarge the bridge-head in front of the newly capturedCAEN. Battalion took over position in area of CAEN from Armed Bde.

5. 20 July-23 July: Battalion attacked and captured FRENOUVILLE.

6. 23 July-28 July: Semi rest area at GIBBERVILLE. Decoy to the German Pz Divs and at notice took part in advance towards BRETTVILLE SUR LAIZE. Gds Armd Divs part cancelled.

7. 28 July: Back to rest area in BAYEUX area.

8. 31 July: Took up advance of Gds Armd Divs with tanks of 2nd ArmdIrish from ST MARTIN to pt 204.

9. 1 August-5August: Advance continued via ST CHARLES DE PERCY to LAMARVINDERE.

10. 6 August-9August: Attack from LAMARVINDERE to LE BUSQ.

11. 9 August-10 August: Move to area pt 218

12. 11 August-12 August: Attack and capture CHENODOLL and out VIRE-VASSY road.

13. 12 August-16 August: Withdrawn back to position by BAS FERIERE: from the enemy withdrew from us via the FALAISE pocket.

14. 16 August-24 August: Rest area MAISONCELLE.

15. 24 August-29 August: Move up to further rest area CONDE SUR NOIREAU.

16. 29 August: Move to area of LAIGLE and stage the night enroute for advance to BRUSSELS.

17. 30 August: Cross River SEINE at VERNON then after a short halt reach GISORS at night (Gds Armd div now in the load).

18. 31 August: Reach the SOMME at CORBIE. Battalion in position guarding bridges.

19. 1 September: With the 1st ArmdColdmGds advanced and captured ARRAS, then on to the high ground to the north. 3 coy under command 2nd Armdirish go on to DOUAI.

20. 2 September: Moved up to behind DOUAI.

21. 3 September: Advance to BRUSSELS following Grenadier GdsGp.

22. 4 September-5 September: Took up position guarding N.W of BRUSSELS.

23. 6 September-7 September: Advance to the ALBERT Canal. Own centre line abandoned. Crossing made at BEERINGEN. Coldm to position S.W of DIEST.

24. 8 September-9 September: Bn expanding bridgehead from BERRINGEN: fought BEVERLOO and HEPPEN west of BOURG LEOPOLD.

25. 9 September-10 September: Advance up to ESCUAT CANAL.

26. 12 September-15 September: Took over the bridgehead advanced to LA COLONIE.

27. 16 September-17 September: Back to rest area behind the Canal at LINDELEI then at NEERPELT.

28. 18 September: Advance to EINDHOVEN. Harboured area of VALKENSWARD.

29. 19 September: Leading Gp of Gds Armd Div reached NIJMEGEN. Bn to area west of MAASTRICHT-WAALWIJK Canal.

30. 20 September-21 September: In counter attack role with 82 U.S Airboune Div.

31. 22 September-25 September: Back down C.L to clear sane of enemy. Battle of VOKEL.

32. 25 September-30 September: Move to join 2 Coy in OSS. Remainder of Bn astride GRAVE-HEESCH Rd.

33. 1 October-2 October: Back under command 82 U.S Airborne, area of MOOK.

34. 2 October-6 October: Took over on the island from 3rd Irish Guards in the area E. of ELST around the hamlet of A.M.

35. 7 October: To rest area W. of MAAS-WAAL Canal.

36. 10 October-3 November: To rest area E. of MAAS-WAAL Canal at HATERT.

37. 4 November-11 November: Bn to defensive position in MAAS pocket, area of LEUNE Here relieved Motor Bn of 11thArmdfor a rest.

38. 11 November-20 December: GdsArmdDiv take over SITTARD sector from U.S Bn in area at WEIR.

39. 21 December: German ARDENNES offensive. Move to area OPHEYLISSEM.

40. 25 December-27 December: Take over protection of bridge at NAMUR.

41. 27 December-7 February: Back to OPHEYLISSM for long rest.

1945

42. 7 February-10 February: To HARLEN, concentration area for operation “VERITABLE”.

43. 11 February-12 February: Closing up to battle, move to NIJMEGEN.

44. 13 February: Closing up to battle, move to GROESBEEK.

45. 14 February-15 February: Under command 51 DIV attack to enlarge GENNEP bridgehead over the NIERS.

46. 16 February-21 February: Second attack. Captured MULLHEIEM.

47. 22 February: Rest area at HOMMERSUM.

48. 23 February-3 March: Took over defensive position N. E of GOCH at SCHULE, prior to and during Canadian advance to UDEM.

49. 4 March: Attacked through Grenadier Gds to Capture METXEKATH

50. 9 March: Attacked through 2nd Scots Gds to WESEAL Bridgehead.

51. 10March-12March: Temporary rest area at METXEKATH.

52. 12 March-28 March: Rest area at MOOK.

53. 29 March: Move to concentration area for operation “PLUNDER”N.E of UDEM.

54. 30 March: Crossed the Rhine at REES and to harbour area

55. 31 March: Coldm Gp start C.L to left and reach NEEDE.

56. 1 April: Coldm Gp cross TWENTE and clear ENSCHEDE

57. 2 April-4 April: Behind SC/WG Gp near DENEKAMP.

58. 3 April-5 April: Follow Scots/Welsh Gp to MITTLELOHNE, W, of R3 Coy capture bridge over the EMS. Operation between river and canal.

59. 6April: Advance from LINGEN to capture REMSE and BACCUM.

60. 7April: Continued advance capturing HANDRUP and out flanking LENGRICH.

61. 8April: Attacked and captured BERGE.

62. 11April: Battle to cross R. HASE and capture BOEN.

63. 13April: Load to VESTRUPT.

64. 14April-17 April: Cleared rest area and settled in at EMSTEK.

65. 17 April: Move across VESSER and ALLER to concentration areaat EILSTORF.

66. 18 April-19 April: Captured NEUNEKIRRCHEN and VISSELHEVODE.

67. 20April: S CHEESSEL surrenders to coldm Gp.

68. 22April: Joint Coldm/scots Gds attack captures ROTTENBURG.

69. 24April: Joint coldm/Gren Gds attack captures ZEVEN.

70. 26April-27 April: ColdmGp move BADENSTEDT then captured WENTEL.

71. 29 April: Move to HOLLENBECK.

72. 30 April: Advance to DIENSTE having cleared HARSFELD.

73. 1 May: 1 Coy into surrendered STADE.

74. 3May: 4 Coy to HIMMELPFORTEN.

75. 4 May: Last act of war. 4 Coy across OSTE Canal and HECHTHAUSEN.

76. 7 May: Move to airfield south of CUXHAVEN to incarcerate 7 para Div

77. 8 May: **V.E DAY.**

AFTERWORD

Grandad, Coldstream Guards Sergeant Stephen Simpson 2664217 was admired greatly and to this day he is remembered with fondness by all who knew him.

The more I researched this book the more respect I have gained for Grandad, his comrades and the military today, particularly the Coldstream Guards.

New threats to our safety and freedom come, our rich cultural society may not have the mind set and loyalty to the monarch that past generations have, the modern soldier does the same job, they protect the innocent from modern atrocities, they do it for their country and for you and me. For this I thank them and I believe they are as important and as heroic and should be admired as much as my Grandad was, he saw it, I see it, can we as a society have An All Seeing Eye too?

ACKNOWLEDGEMENTS

With thanks to Coldstream Guardsman Scott Taylor, Regimental Archivist at Wellington Barracks; for his courtesy, help and support of Grandad's War.

With thanks to (Veteran of Northern Ireland) Coldstream Guardsman Phil Lee, for contributing to the interview process and Grandad's story, whilst treating Grandad with great respect.

Phil Lee on left with Steve during secondary interview.

With special thanks to Ian Reynolds and his continuous support throughout the project.

With thanks to Charles Simpson, (Steve's Grandson) for his passionate support and great contributions to the book throughout the project.

With thanks to Stephen Simpson (Steve's son) for his support and for allowing the use of Grandad's valuable collection of artefacts.

BIBLIOGRAPHY

Borne A.C, Distinctions Honorifiques de la Belgique 1830 – 1985, Published (1985)

Coldstream Guards 5th Battalion Official War Diary 1939 – 1945, Coldstream Guards HQ Wellington Barracks Archives

Coldstream Guards, 'The Brussels Sprout' No.33 Edition, Friday 11th May 1945

History Learning Site; www.historylearningsite.co.uk

http://www.bbc.co.uk/history/ww2peopleswar/stories/58/a7208958.shtml

O'Neill William, The Oxford Essential Guide to World War II, Published Berkley Books (2002)

Smith Bruce, 'Tireless Worker for ex-army comrades dies, 85', Yorkshire Evening Post, Leeds 13th April (2009)

The War In Pictures; Fifth Year Oldham's Press Limited London, Printed by Alabaster, Passmor & Sons Ltd (1945)

The War In Pictures; Sixth Year Oldham's Press Limited London Printed by Alabaster, Passmor & Sons Ltd (1945)

Zeller Alan http:// www.5thbncoldstreamguards.com 2015 History of the 5th Btn Coldstream Guards

AUTHOR BIOGRAPHY

A C Reynolds is a freelance writer and artist, offering Ghost-writing services for life stories. Amanda has studied at Bradford University; Human Behaviour, counselling, literature, creative writing and specialises in life trauma's and PTSD.

If you think you have an interesting story to tell, contact Amanda for an informal chat about your military career or life story.

Please visit www.amandareynolds.co.uk for more details.

Email grandadswar@yahoo.com.

Follow Amanda on twitter @ACRDesign

or Facebook: Grandads War Pages.